Three Steps to Awakening

Three Steps to Awakening

OSHO

PAN

This edition published 2019 by Pan
an imprint of Pan Macmillan Publishing India Private Limited,
707, Kailash Building
26 K. G. Marg, New Delhi – 110 001
www.panmacmillan.co.in

Pan Macmillan, The Smithson, 6 Briset Street, London EC1M 5NR,
Basingstoke and Oxford
Associated companies throughout the world
www.panmacmillan.com

ISBN 978-93-89109-10-8

Originally published in Hindi under the title *Samadhi Ke Teen Charan*

Photos of Osho: Courtesy OSHO International Foundation

The material in this book is a transcript originally published in Hindi as Samadhi Ke Teen Charan,. given to a live audience. All of Osho's talks have been published in full as books, and are also available as original audio recordings. Audio recordings and the complete text archive can be found via the online OSHO Library at www.osho.com/library

5 7 9 8 6

Typeset by Manmohan Kumar
Printed and bound in India at Repro India Ltd., Mumbai

FSC www.fsc.org
MIX
Paper from responsible sources
FSC® C047271

Contents

Preface

Waking up or awakening means that the dream is over – whatever was known up to now remains no longer. So it is difficult to say what awakening means, because your language is of sleep. At present, whatever can be told to you or whatever can be understood by you will be in the language of the dream. If I say that you will get happiness, then you will think of the happiness which you have known in the dream. If I say that you will not get misery, then you will think of the same misery which you have known in the dream.

If you think, you will not attain. That is why all the buddhas have kept quiet. Whenever someone asked what will happen after the awakening they just kept quiet. They said, "Wake up and see," because this is beyond the language which you know, or this is beyond your understanding which you have through language. Neither your happiness nor your misery is there. Neither your peace nor your restlessness is there. Neither your satisfaction nor your dissatisfaction – whatever you have known up to now is not there. The scriptures you have known up to now are also not there. The images of the divine which were made by you are also not there. Your notions about heaven and hell are also not there. When you are not there, your notions also will not be there.

There is something which cannot be described, which cannot be defined – you can call it *brahman, Vishnupad, jinpad* or buddhahood, but even by these words nothing can be known. If you wake up, only then can you know. A dumb man cannot describe the taste of sugar, but he can enjoy it.

What will happen after awakening? You will taste the divine, the taste which you have been trying to get all these past lives but could not get – you missed it always. It just cannot be described. If you are bored with the way you have been living, then wake up. But if you have not even a little bit of interest in it yet, then just turn over and go to sleep again.

But you will have to wake up one day. Sleep cannot be eternal, and sleep cannot be the ultimate rest, and darkness cannot be the experience of the ultimate truth. Sooner or later you will have to get up – it all depends on you. But whenever you awaken you will repent for not having woken up earlier – it just meant spreading out your hand – it was so near.

Osho
The Song of Ecstasy

Introduction

Every few thousand years an individual appears who irrevocably changes the world around him in ways that are never immediately apparent, except to the most perceptive.

Osho is one such individual: his spoken words will resonate for centuries to come.

All those words have been recorded and transcribed into books like this one; written words that can carry a transforming message to the reader.

For Osho, all change is individual. There is no 'society' to change – it can only happen to each one of us, one at a time. So, no matter what the subject matter of the book, the thread that runs through all Osho's words is like a love song that we can suddenly, mysteriously, hear at just the right moment. And strangely, no matter what the words seem to be referring to, they are really only referring to us.

And this is no ordinary love song; it is more an invitation to open our hearts to hear something beyond the words, beyond the heart...a silence beyond all understanding. Where we all belong.

1
Freedom of Consciousness

I am thinking about what subject I should speak to you on. There are so many topics and the world is filled with so many issues that this hesitation is very natural. There are many schools of thought, theologies, and doctrines about truth. I fear that my talks could even increase the burden that is already very heavy on humanity. I feel very hesitant, afraid to say anything because it may stick in your mind. I'm afraid you may cling to what is being said, afraid you may find what I am going to say very appealing, and that it might make a place for itself in your mind.

Man is troubled and in anguish because of thoughts and doctrines. It is because of doctrines that truth is never born in the life of man. Borrowed knowledge and what others say are always within him, and they are a hindrance for the truth. Knowledge is not attained from the outside; whatever is gathered from the outside holds back the truth.

I am also outside of you. Whatever I say will also be from the outside; you should not think of it as knowledge. It is not knowledge; it cannot be knowledge for you. Whatever someone else gives you cannot be your knowledge and there is even a danger that it could cover up your ignorance. Your ignorance can be covered up, hidden, and you may start to feel you know something.

When you hear something about truth, you feel that you have known the truth. After reading about truth, you think that you have known it, and so you become handicapped and incapable of attaining the truth.

First, let me tell you that whatever comes from the outside can never be your knowing. Of course, someone could then ask me why I am speaking. Why am I saying anything? I am outside and I am saying something. The only thing I want to say is, take whatever comes from the outside as being outside of yourself; don't consider it your knowing. Whether it comes from me or from someone else does not matter.

Knowing is the true self-nature of every human being. And to know that self-nature, we do not need to search outside. If we want to know what is within us, whatever we have learned on the outside has to be unlearned, has to be left aside.

Those who want to know the truth have to put the scriptures aside. Whoever clings to scriptures cannot attain the truth. And all of us are clinging to scriptures; all the trouble in the world is due to clinging to scriptures. Who are the Hindus, the Muslims, the Jainas, the Christians, or the Parsees? What is making them fight against each other? What is separating them from one another?

It is the scriptures that separate them. It is the scriptures that make them fight with each other. The whole of mankind is divided because some people cling to certain books, and others cling to other books. Books have become so valuable that we can kill because of them. In the past three thousand years, we have killed millions of people because books are so valuable. Because books have become worthy of worship, even the godliness that exists inside man can be demeaned, it can even be rejected, it can even be deadened. That is what has happened, and that is happening even today.

The wall between one man and another is made of religious scriptures. Does it ever occur to you to ask how the scriptures, which separate one man from another, could ever join man with existence? How could that which separates man from man become a ladder to connect man to existence? We think that perhaps we will find something in the scriptures. And we do find something in them; we find words. We find words that define the truth, and we memorize those words. They enter our memory and we think that memory is knowledge.

Memory is not knowledge. To learn something and to memorize it is not knowing. The birth of knowing is a very different thing. Knowing revolutionizes your whole life. The training of memory is something else; with the training of memory someone can become a pundit, but it does not awaken wisdom.

I am not going to commit a sin by giving you a lecture. All those who give discourses are violent and commit sin. I am not going to give you a discourse. I am here only to share a few things with you. Not because you should believe them; anyone who says you should believe is your enemy. Anyone who says to have faith, anyone who says to have a belief is fatal to you; he stops your life from growing. Anyone who says to have faith is a hindrance in awakening your intelligence.

We have been believers for a very long time, and our world today is the result of all that believing. Can there be a more rotten world than this? More corrupt? We are people who are believers, and we have been believing for a very long time. Can man be worse than he is today? Can our brains be more rotten than they are today? Can there be more pain and tension and anguish than there is today? We have had beliefs for a long time, and the whole world believes – some people in this temple, some in that mosque, some in that church; some in this book, some in another book; someone in this prophet, someone in that prophet. The whole world believes. In spite of all that believing, our world is the result.

Some people may say that this is due to a lack of belief. I want to say to you, may existence erase all those beliefs completely. If belief were to become total, man would be finished – because his intelligence would be destroyed. Belief is anti-intelligence. Whenever someone says you should believe what he says, what he is actually saying is that you do not need to walk with your own feet. Whenever someone says to have faith, he is saying, "Why do you need eyes? I have eyes."

I have read a short story…

There was a man in a village who lost his eyesight. He was an old man. He was a very old man; he was around ninety years old. All the members of his family – and he had eight sons – all eight sons told him to get his eyes treated. They told him the doctors said that his eyes could be cured.

The old man said, "Why do I need eyes? I have eight sons, and they have sixteen eyes. They have eight wives who have sixteen eyes. There are thirty-two eyes to see for me; why do I need eyes? For what? I can live like a blind man."

His sons told him again and again but to no avail. The old man did not agree. He said, "Why do I need to have eyes? There are thirty-two eyes in my house."

Days went by. One day their house caught fire. The thirty-two eyes went outside, and the old man was left inside. The house was on fire, the old man was left in the house, and the thirty-two eyes ran outside. Then he remembered that only one's own eyes are of any help; no one else's eyes can be of any help.

It is only one's own intelligence that is of any use; beliefs given by others do not help. In life, fire surrounds us, all the time. We are surrounded by the fire of life twenty-four hours a day.

It is only our own eyes that can help us, not someone else's – neither Mahavira's, nor Buddha's, nor Krishna's, nor Rama's. Someone else's eyes cannot help us.

But the priests, the merchants selling religion, the people who exploit in the name of religion, are preaching to have faith: "What is the need of intelligence? Why do you need to think for yourself? Thoughts are already available. Divine thoughts are available; you should believe in them."

We have believed in those thoughts, but we have been falling lower and lower. Our consciousness has been continually going downward. No consciousness can rise upward through belief. Belief is suicide. I do not tell you to believe in something; I tell you to free yourself from all beliefs.

Someone who wants to experience truth, who wants to come close to godliness, who longs to experience the light and love of the divine, should remember that the first condition is to be free of all types of beliefs. Freedom, the freedom of consciousness, the freedom of intelligence, is the first condition for knowing the truth. Someone whose consciousness is not free can know about everything else, but he can never come to know the truth. The freedom of consciousness is essential for entering the door of truth.

Beliefs are binding factors, they make you slaves. Faiths create bondage, they make you slaves. Scriptures and doctrines create bondage and make you slaves. It is surprising: you are born in a certain house – and by chance it is the house of a Hindu or a Muslim – and you are given a faith by birth. For the rest of your life you will say, "I am a Hindu; I am a Muslim; I am a Christian; I am a Jaina." Can knowledge be acquired through birth? Does blood have any relation to knowledge? Can a residence have any relationship to knowledge? If people could become religious just by where they are born, the whole world would have been religious by now. Since the world is so irreligious, it is proof that religion cannot have any relationship to birth – but we have all acquired religion through birth. Acquiring religion through birth is the root cause of the problem. It is because of this that religion is not able to descend upon the earth.

No man is religious through birth, he becomes religious through life. No one can have a faith or a belief through birth. Before our intelligence can be awakened, our society, our family, our parents, teachers, and preachers tie us down with beliefs. Before our intelligence can fly in the open sky, the chains of beliefs pull it down and tie it to the earth. We go on limping in those chains for the rest of our lives. We are never able to think. A man who has a belief can never think, because he is always looking from the point of view of his belief. Whatever he thinks is prejudiced. Whatever he thinks is bound by his preconceptions. Whatever thoughts he has are always borrowed and false. They are not his individual thoughts.

A thought that is not one's own, an intelligence that is not one's own, is false. It does not have any truth in it; it does not have any real basis on which life can be built.

What I have been asking people all over the country is, "You have a lot of beliefs; do you also have any thoughts?" They answer, "We have a lot of thoughts." I ask, "Are any one of them yours? Your own? Or do they all come from others?"

Can the wealth that belongs to others give vitality to your life? All the wealth of our thinking is borrowed from others, and belongs to others. That is the first slavery of the mind. The mind should first become free of that slavery. The birth of a new man becomes possible only when his mind becomes free from all borrowed thoughts and concepts. I call freedom the foremost element.

Those who want to move into the search for truth, in whom a thirst is awakening to know the meaning of life, in whom there is a yearning to know the purpose of this vast existence and everything all around us... Those who want to know what that ecstasy is, what that bliss is, and what godliness is, should remember that the first condition, the first introduction, is to move their consciousness toward freedom, to free their consciousness. If they would like to have ultimate freedom, they will have to lay the foundations of freedom in the very first step.

We are all bound; all of us are bound to one belief or another. Why are we bound? We are bound because in order to know, we have to have courage and make an effort.

To believe, there is no need to have courage or make an effort. To have a belief, there is no need to make any kind of effort; there is no need to do any spiritual discipline. To have faith in someone, you need to be extremely lacking in courage, lacking in effort, lacking in discipline. You need to be deeply lazy and have a tendency toward inertia; then belief comes very naturally. Whoever does not wish to search for himself believes in what others say, takes for granted that what they say must be right.

It is the people who have no reverence for truth, who have faith in the common doctrines about truth; someone who has no real thirst for truth easily believes in thoughts that have been given by others. If someone has a true longing for truth, he will not be confined by any religion, any doctrine, or any sect. He will search, he will find out for himself. He will search with all his life energy – and the man who searches in this way will definitely find it. The one who continues to believe not only misses the opportunity of living, he also does not find truth.

The attainment of truth demands effort and discipline. But we start believing; we are scared, frightened people. We fall at anyone's feet. We hold anyone's hand and want to get an explanation of life. We want to cross the river and be lifted up with the help of any guru, any holy man, any saint. That is impossible. That is absolutely impossible; there is nothing more impossible than that.

Freedom is the essential condition of consciousness.

How can our consciousness be free? How can we free and release our consciousness? How can we bring a mind that is bound, imprisoned in patterns, out of the prison? I would like to discuss this extensively with you in three or four sessions. The greatest problem that human beings face is the release and freedom of their consciousness. The question is not about a God, the question is about the freedom of consciousness.

People come and ask me if there is a God. I tell them, "Forget about God; tell me, is your consciousness free?" If someone asks me if there is a sky, if someone asks me if there is a sun, what should I tell him? I would ask him, "Are your eyes open?" The sun exists, but the question is whether his eyes are open or not. The sun exists, but to see the sun you must have open eyes. Godliness exists, but the consciousness has to be open for godliness to come into being. How can a confined mind and closed eyes see it?

A person who is obsessed with belief has closed eyes and a constrained mind. When someone has made up his mind about a point of view, he already has some kind of concept; before getting to know, his mind is already closed. He has shut his doors. Then he asks, "Is there a God? Does truth exist?"

For a closed mind, there is certainly no truth or any God. The real question is not whether God exists or not, nor whether there is a soul or not, nor whether truth exists or not. The real problem is, does that person have a consciousness which can know? Without that consciousness there never has been, and never will be, a way to attain life or to know the meaning of life. Only someone whose intelligence is totally free and has gained the ability to perceive is capable of knowing.

How can we take our consciousness toward the ultimate

liberation? How to open its doors? How to open its windows so the light of the sun can enter in? How to open our eyes so we can see that which is? Whenever we start to believe in something, our eyes are covered with a curtain, and we are not able to see that which is; instead, we start to see what we believe.

There are people who have had a vision of Krishna or a vision of Rama or a vision of Christ. Those visions are possible. If we start to believe in something; if we have faith and give it prominence in our mind; if we continue to remember it, think of it and hypnotize ourselves continuously with it by fasting and doing penance; if we constantly think about it; if we become obsessed with it with constant thought and belief; then we can have a vision. That vision will not be of the truth, it will be only the manifestation of our imagination. It will be only a vision of our thoughts. It will be only the projection of our beliefs. It will be our own dream, to which we have given birth. Throughout the world, people of different religions have different visions. Those visions are not real.

To come face-to-face with real truth as it is, to know godliness as it is, we must let go of all our concepts and imaginations, let all our imaginations evaporate, all our thoughts disappear, and be able to look without any beliefs inside. A vision that is free of belief is a vision of truth. A vision based on belief is the projection of our imagination, a vision of our imagination. That type of vision is not a religious vision; that type of vision is the projection of mental imagination and dreams. That experience is not real; it has been prepared and manufactured by the mind itself. It is mind-created; we have produced it ourselves.

Many people have had such a vision of God. It is not a vision of God because God does not have any form or shape. The truth does not have any form or attributes. To know the truth that pervades everything, we have to become fully silent and empty in every way.

If our consciousness is absolutely choiceless, peaceful and simple, if no thoughts are flowing in our mind, if no dreams are arising in it… If our consciousness is completely silent, in that silence, what will we know?

In that silence, something is known. In that emptiness, a connection and a contact is made with something. In that peace, contact is established with a divine state. That contact, that connection, that understanding, that awareness, that perception is the perception of godliness and truth.

In order to achieve that, as I have said, the first essential step is that the consciousness should be free. The mind must be free of belief; the dust of sects and doctrines should be detached and swept away.

We are obsessed and filled with the burden of thoughts, doctrines, and scriptures that rest upon us. We are crushed by them. For the past five thousand years human beings have been thinking and the weight of those five thousand years of thought rests on the brain of one small person. The weight of all the cultivated thoughts of five thousand years rests on us. Because of that burden, our consciousness is not able to be free, not able to rise upward. Whenever we start to think, we start to go round and round within that weight. There are grooves, and we just turn around in those grooves. Our mind goes round and round just like a tethered buffalo that keeps on going round and round the same well.

Before anyone can enter the unknown world of truth, it is essential for him to leave all his known ways. He must drop all that he knows, so that knowing can be born. He must remove all that he believes, so that he can see what is.

You must have seen a reservoir filled with water; it is filled with water that comes from the outside. It is built by joining bricks in a circle with cement and pouring water into it from the outside. On the other hand you also must have seen water in a well. There, all the stones and mud are removed, and a spring of water rises up from underneath. The water in the reservoir will go bad in a few days. It is stagnant. The water in the well, which has a spring at its source, will not go bad. The well has a very deep connection with its life springs, where there is a lot of water; they are ultimately connected with the sea. The reservoir is not connected to anything; water coming from the outside fills it up. The well is ultimately connected with the ocean; it is not filled with anything from the outside.

There are also two types of knowledge. One is the knowledge of the reservoir, which is filled from the outside. It becomes rotten very soon. No brain in the world is more rotten than the brain of the pundit. He becomes incapable of right thinking. His state is a very crippled one. Everything inside him has been filled from the outside. He just keeps repeating it; he is like a machine. A pundit's lectures are very mechanical. You can ask him anything; the answer is already there. Before you can ask him a question, inside he already knows the solution. He knows the answer. The answers have been stuffed into him from the outside.

In the West these days, and soon in our country also, they have invented machines into which you can put questions, and the machines will give answers. Then there will be no need for pundits in the world, because there are machines in which the questions and answers have been fed beforehand. You can feed in the questions and say you want the answer to the fifth question, and the machine will give you the answer. The machine will tell you what the answer is, so there is no need for any pundit in the world; a machine can do his work more efficiently. With machines there is also one more benefit; they do not make anyone fight with anyone else, they do not create any conflict. They do not make one pundit stand up against another pundit. They do not dispute. They only give the answer.

Knowledge that has been fed in from the outside is fatal. It does not free the brain; it conditions the brain and makes it fragmented. It breaks its possibility to fly, it destroys its wings.

Another kind of knowledge comes from within, just like the water of the well. In a well you have to remove the mud and stones, and in a reservoir you have to cement the mud and stones together. In one the water springs up by itself, the other you have to fill with water. The process of building those two is certainly different; it is opposite to one another.

Do you gather knowledge from the outside like a reservoir? If you do, you must be careful; you are destroying your intelligence with your own hands. You are tying your brain – which can fly toward the divine – to the ground.

Do not gather knowledge from the outside. Let knowing come from the inside. For knowing to come from the inside, you must remove all the mud and stones you have gathered. Remove all the information you have gathered and become simple. If you remove the information and become simple, you will find a new energy arising within you. Something new will start to come into being.

It is easy to give up wealth and difficult to give up thoughts. It is very difficult to drop thoughts; you will certainly wonder how you can remove them. When a man becomes a monk, he gives up wealth, renounces his house, renounces his friends and relatives, and gives up his wife and friends. But he does not drop the thoughts to which he was clinging as a householder. He keeps on clinging to them. If he was a Jaina, he says, "I am a Jaina monk." If he was a Muslim, he says, "I am a Muslim monk." If he was a Christian, he says, "I am a Christian monk." He continues to cling to the thoughts he had been clinging to, and renounces everything else. The household that he renounced lies outside himself. The thoughts of the householder are inside him, and it is difficult to give them up.

Whoever gives up his thoughts is capable of knowing the truth. Merely by renouncing his house, no one can come to know the truth; the walls of a house are not barriers to knowing the truth. Whether I am sitting in one house or in another house, the walls are not barriers to knowing the truth. The person I am sitting with is also not a barrier. The place I am in is also not a barrier. There is only one barrier to knowing the truth, and that is the wall of thoughts inside; that alone is the hindrance.

Destroying it is certainly difficult. When I say you should drop your thoughts, the question arises, how to drop them? How can thoughts go away? They are constantly inside. How can you forget what you have learned?

There is certainly a way to forget whatever we have learned. There is a way to disperse what has been gathered. There is a way to release what has been packed inside, and it is the same method that was used to bring it inside. The method is always the same. We use the steps we have climbed up to go back down. The method is always the same, going and coming do not make any difference to the method. There is only a difference of direction; the only difference is to turn our face around.

All the methods used to gather thoughts can be dispersed by turning our face in the opposite direction. How have we gathered thoughts? The most important and deepest layer of gathering thoughts is our attachment. It is the feeling that they are ours. It feels as though the thoughts are ours.

Does any thought belong to you? If I start to argue, you will say, "My thoughts are correct." Just think a little, is any thought yours? Or have all thoughts come from the outside?

It is pointless to say that a thought is "mine." Even religious people who say, "The wife is not mine, the children are not mine, the house is not mine," claim, "This is my religion." Even they say, "My thought, my philosophy." Even they are not able to drop attachment at the level of thought. Their feeling of "mine" does not go away. Those who cannot drop the feeling of attachment at that level cannot let go of their feeling of attachment at any level. No matter how many times they might say, "The wife is not mine," deep down they will feel, "She is my wife."

Swami Ramateertha returned from America. He had been teaching all over Europe and America about the true essence of things, and he had acquired a lot of influence. Millions of people had heard him and worshipped him. He came back to India and spent some days in the Himalayas. His wife went to meet him, and Ramateertha refused to meet with her. He said, "I will not meet her."

Sardar Pooran Singh, who was living with him, was very surprised. He said to Ramateertha, "I have never seen you refuse to meet a woman. In Europe and America, thousands of women came and you never refused to meet any of them. Why are you refusing to meet this woman? At some level do you still believe her to be your wife? You left her and went away. You are refusing to meet your own wife."

Definitely, at some level he still believed her to be his wife – other women visited him and he never refused to meet them.

As long as you have an attachment to thoughts, you should not be under the illusion that you can drop anything. The real clinging and burden is that of thought. Everything else is on the outside, it does not have a hold on you. It is only thought that has a hold on you. It is the circle of thought, the heavy load of thought through which you feel you know something. It is worth asking yourself, "Is any of it really mine?"

Once there was a famous monk. A young seeker came to visit his commune. For a few days the young seeker listened to what the old monk had to say – and the old monk had very little to say. The young seeker got tired of listening to the same things again and again, and he thought, "I had better leave this commune, it seems there is nothing much to learn here."

Just then a new monk entered the commune. That night the new monk gave a great discourse, which was wonderful, very serious, subtle, and deep.

The young seeker listened to the talk of the visiting monk, the guest, and said to himself, "This is what a master should be like; he has such great knowledge, so serious and deep. The old monk in whose commune I am staying knows only a few things, nothing more." He also thought that the old monk must have felt sad when he listened to the new monk speaking like that. He must have felt insulted. "The old monk does not know anything; he has wasted his life."

After completing his talk, the monk looked around the assembly very proudly to see the impression he made on them. He also looked at the old monk.

The old monk said, "I have been listening very attentively for the past two hours, but I saw that you did not speak at all."

The monk said, "Are you mad? I have been speaking for the last two hours, and everyone else was silent – and you say you listened to me for two hours and I have not said anything?"

The old monk said, "I have certainly listened very carefully to you, but you never said anything. Whatever you said was completely taken from others. You had no thoughts from your own experience. That is why I say you never said anything. Others were speaking through you, but you did not speak."

For freedom of thought, for liberation of thought, and for the awakening of intelligence, the first thing, the first awareness that is needed is: "No thought is mine. No thought is mine." Calling a thought "mine" which is not your own is lying.

No thought is "yours." You should break the identification with thoughts.

We start to identify ourselves with every thought. We say, "The Jaina religion is mine; the Hindu religion is mine; Rama is mine; Krishna is mine; Christ is mine." We start to identify ourselves with thoughts.

And this is surprising because no thought is yours. No religion is yours. Establish the awareness that "no thought is mine" inside your intelligence. Spread out all your thoughts and see that they have all come from somewhere. Just like the birds descend on the trees in the evening to roost, thoughts also come in the same way to the mind to roost. You are just like a guesthouse where people come and go.

I remember a story that took place at a small inn...

People were arriving at the inn to stay the night. Another group of people, who had finished their work, were leaving. A mystic was sitting outside the inn and laughing. A man who had just arrived asked the mystic, "Why are you laughing?"

He replied, "Looking at this inn reminds me of my mind; that is why I am laughing."

In the same way, thoughts come and go. The mind is only an inn, and no thought belongs to it. The mind is only an inn where thoughts come and go.

Observe your mind carefully, and you will come to know. The thoughts you had yesterday are not there today; the thoughts of the day before are not there today; the thoughts you had a year ago, you do not have today; the thoughts you had ten years ago are not there today; and there is no sign today of the thoughts of twenty years ago. Whether you are fifty years old or forty years old, or thirty years old, or twenty years old, just look back: How many of the thoughts that have passed through your mind during those twenty years remain today? Thoughts have come and gone. You are only an inn, a place to rest. By mistake you count the thoughts as yours. And as you start to think that they are yours, the thoughts begin to have a hold on you, and the wall of thoughts starts to build up.

The first thing you must remember for the freedom of consciousness is to know that no thought is yours. If no thought is yours and thoughts come and go, who are you? Who are you in that case? You are certainly no more than a witness. You are certainly no more than just an observer. You are only a watcher.

Even watching a play we get identified. Even watching a film we become identified. The film is going on and an unhappy scene takes place, and we start crying – and this does not apply only to ordinary people.

In Bengal there was a great thinker, Ishwar Chandra Vidyasagar. He was thought to be a fountain of knowledge. A small play was being staged in Kolkata, and he went to watch it. In that play there was a character who was supposed to be abusive and violent toward a woman, and he started to abuse and tease her. Vidyasagar, who was watching the play, became so angry with the actor that he took off his shoe and flung it at him – and he was thought to be a fountain of knowledge! He threw his shoe and hit the actor.

The actor must have been wiser than him. He picked up the shoe, took a bow, and said, "My acting has been so successful that I have managed to deceive even such a great man as you." He said, "This will be my trophy for life. I have never received a greater reward for my acting than this. It means that I have succeeded in my art."

Later on, Vidyasagar felt very embarrassed, and he said, "How could I have made such a mistake? I completely forgot that it was supposed to be only a play, and I identified myself with it."

In this life, even at the level of thought we are no more than an observer – but we identify ourselves with our thoughts. We are only a witness to the thoughts that come and go on the screen of the mind.

Just remember... In the night you had a dream, and in the morning you woke up. You commented that dreams come and go, and then you went through the day. You were a child and you went through childhood; you became a young man; you became old. Just try to remember; what is the eternal element inside you that has been continually present? What has been continually present?

Except for the witness, nothing else remains. Everything else comes and goes. Childhood comes and goes; youth comes and goes; old age comes and passes away. Birth happens, death happens; happiness takes place, unhappiness takes place; sunshine comes, shade comes; respect happens, insult happens. All these things come and go.

What is the one element in the whole of life that never comes and never goes? It is only the element of the witness. It cannot be anything else that observes all these things, that observes that the sun has come, that notices the sun has gone, that observes youth has come, that observes old age has come, that sees a thought has come and watches that another thought has passed. Except for the thread of the witness, everything inside you just comes and goes. No other element remains. Only one thing remains, and that is the power to see, the capability to observe and to be the observer, the state of the witness.

Be a witness at the level of thought. Observe the thought, don't cling to it. Don't cling to the thought, observe it. Observe it just as a witness.

We are not able to be a witness because we believe that some thoughts are bad and some are good. We want to cling to the good ones and push away the bad ones and that is why we are not able to become a witness. The man who differentiates between good and bad thoughts – this thought is good, and he wants to cling to the good thought and remove the bad thought… The man who differentiates between the good and the bad cannot be a witness.

A thought is only a thought; a thought is neither good nor bad. A thought is neither good nor bad; a thought is only a thought. The moment someone starts to say good or bad, he clings to one and pushes away the other. Moreover, someone who clings to one and tries to drop the other should understand that what he calls good and what he calls bad are two sides of the same coin. If he clings to the good, the bad will also survive – and someone who pushes away the bad, pushes away the good also. They are joined together.

Thoughts are joined together. You should not believe that the man we call good has no bad thoughts. He does have bad thoughts. You cannot find a good man who does not have some bad thoughts, and you cannot find a bad man who does not have good thoughts.

Yes, the man who has absolutely no thoughts certainly exists. That is a completely different thing, a totally different thing; I am not talking about that just now. Such a person, without thoughts, does exist. He is neither good nor bad. He has risen above man; he has transcended good and evil. I call him a mystic. Only he knows the truth.

The man who clings to the good should remember that the bad still exists inside. You will be surprised to know that what a bad man does in his waking hours, a good man does in his sleep, because a good man has bad thoughts inside. And you will be very surprised to know that bad men do not have bad dreams; it is the good man who has bad dreams. A bad man has good dreams. A bad man dreams of being a saint, and a good man dreams of being bad. What they cling to in their waking hours and have pushed down while awake comes back when they are unconscious. It was present, but they did not allow it to manifest when they were awake. It manifests in unconsciousness.

If you were to open the minds of good men, in their minds they would be doing all the sins that the people who are locked up in prisons do. There is not much difference between them. A good man also does all the sins that a bad man does. He does them in his mind, and the bad man does them on the outside. In their imagination, bad men continue to do all the good things that a good man does. They continue to dream about them. Good and bad always stay together. There is no such thing as a good man who does not have a bad side to him. Similarly, there is no bad man who does not also have a good side to him.

What we repress goes underneath; what we emphasize comes up. It is just like a coin; when heads faces up, tails faces down. In the same way, good and bad are two sides of the same thought.

Someone who wants to be a witness and wants to know the truth has to understand that all thoughts are just thoughts. Nothing is good and nothing is bad. When someone decides something is good and something is bad, he clings to one and tries to drop the other, and cannot remain a witness. To be a witness you must remain nonjudgmental, in a state without any judgment, desire, or imagination. That means to be in a state where you don't project anything, where you see thoughts exactly as they are. A man who is just a witness of thoughts and does not judge, does not think them to be good or bad, has no condemnation, does not criticize or praise any thought, will be very surprised; continuing to observe like this, silently, serene, just a witness, he will slowly, slowly find that his thoughts have disappeared, his thoughts have become empty. Thoughts stop coming to the consciousness of someone who drops all feelings of attachment to his thoughts.

By feelings of attachment, I mean that he drops love and hate toward them altogether. Both are feelings of attachment. The one we love comes to our door, and the one we hate comes to our door as well. Friends continue to surround us, and enemies also continue to surround us. It might happen that sometimes we are not surrounded by friends, but enemies always surround us. Our mind continues to be obsessed by them.

If someone thinks that money is bad, that thinking of money is bad, he will find himself filled with thoughts of money around the clock. If someone starts to think that food is bad and that it is not right to eat, he will be thinking of food all the time. If someone starts to think that sex is a sin, sexual desire is a sin, and starts to fight with it, he will find his mind obsessed with the thought of sex. The thought against which you fight accepts your invitation; whatever you fight with starts to come. It is the law of the mind that what you fight with will be invited. What you have pushed away will start to come just because of your pushing.

That is why thoughts are neither to be fought with nor to be praised, neither to be clung to nor to be pushed away. They are simply to be observed. It requires great courage because a bad thought will come and you will feel like pushing it away, and a good thought will also come and your mind will feel like clinging to it. If you remember to meditate with awareness and mindfulness on this tendency of the mind to cling and to push away, it will slowly, slowly fade away, and you will become capable of observing thought. Whoever is capable of observing thought is capable of being liberated from thought. Whoever is capable of witnessing thought is capable of being free from thought.

You do not observe the flow of thoughts. You never stop and pause to watch what is going on inside. Maybe you have never even sat down for half an hour to observe what is going on inside you. It is going on, and you continue what you are doing; it is going on, and you go on working; it is going on, and you continue to eat; it is going on, and you continue to run your shop; it is going on, you continue to write, you continue to speak; it is going on while I am speaking and you are listening. It is continually going on inside. It goes on continually by itself. Slowly, slowly you have stopped even bothering about what is going on inside you. You continue to do your own thing. That is why you are almost asleep. Inside, the mind is doing one thing, and you are doing something else. You are absent. You are not present toward yourself. You are not awake toward yourself.

Someone once asked Mahavira, "What kind of man is wise?"

Mahavira replied, "One who is awake is wise, and one who is asleep is not wise." It is a unique statement, a very unique statement – the one who is asleep.

All of us are asleep. All of us are completely asleep toward what is going on inside us. Our very interiority is our real being, and we are unaware of it. We are awake to what is going on outside, to what is happening outside. We are awake to what is happening outside; we are asleep toward what is going on inside. That is the suffering of life, and that is the ignorance of life; that is the slavery of life, and that is its bondage.

We have to awaken to what is going on inside. Someone who is aware of the whole flow of thoughts, sees it, understands it and remains a witness, passes through a very unique experience. He starts to experience that all the thoughts he witnesses without attachment stop coming. All the thoughts he is capable of observing become incapable of coming, and a moment comes when there are no thoughts left. What is left is intelligence.

A time comes when there are no thoughts and you are there. What is awakened in you is free intelligence, liberated intelligence. It is that free intelligence that is capable of knowing the truth. A fettered intelligence is incapable of knowing the truth.

Freedom is the first requisite. You will have to sharpen that freedom. Without sharpening it, no progress can be made as far as freedom is concerned. No matter how many scriptures you may read, or doctrines you may understand or even memorize, you will be memorizing only words; nothing else will happen. The words will occupy your brain. Possessing too many words is not a sign of knowledge. Mad people are stuffed with words, even more than you. Words are not a sign of knowledge.

One more thing you should know is that if your mind is too stuffed with words, you can go crazy. There is not much difference between an ordinary man and a madman. An ordinary man has fewer words inside, and a madman has more words inside.

Everyone is standing on the brink of madness. Just a little push and you can go mad. If the words inside start buzzing loudly, you can go mad. Now psychologists are saying that one out of three people is on the verge of madness. One out of three! That means that out of all the people present here, one-third are on the verge of madness. Do not think that it is your neighbor who is in this condition and not you; that is a sign you are in trouble. If you think your neighbor is mad, it means you are in trouble – because no madman ever thinks he is mad. He always thinks the other is mad. One of the essential signs of a mad person is that he always thinks others are mad. You cannot convince a mad person that he is mad. If he understands that much, it is proof he is not mad.

Almost all of us are reaching that state. These days in America, one and a half million people consult a psychologist about their mental state every day. Those are official figures. Another million and a half must be consulting private doctors also, so about three million people consult psychologists every day. Why do they seek advice? They have too many thoughts, and slowly, slowly the thoughts become so overpowering that they lose control over themselves. They do not know what to do; their thoughts move so intensely that they lose control over their lives.

You should consider this and think about it carefully for yourself also. Are your thoughts overpowering? Sit down for ten minutes and write down honestly whatever thought comes to your mind. Don't leave out anything. Whatever comes; if an incomplete thought comes, write it down incomplete; if a complete thought comes, write it down complete. For ten minutes write down everything that comes to your mind, and then show it to someone. He will ask you, "What madman has written this?" You can show it to anyone, and he will ask you, "Who is the madman who has written this?" Actually, you yourself will understand what madman has written it. If you were to bring out everything that goes on inside you and look at it for ten minutes, you yourself would become worried about what kind of madman you are, what is going on, what is happening in you. We never stop and look at what is happening in us – and we think we are great thinkers. All madmen think that.

You know well that those who reach the very extreme of thinking go mad. For the past fifty years, almost all the great thinkers in Europe have gone mad. Most of them have spent some time in a mental asylum at one time or another in their life. It seems that a thinker who does not become mad must not be that great a thinker. A time will come when we will think that any thinker who has not been to a mental asylum is not a great thinker. That is also right. The ultimate result of thinking is madness. That is why I do not call Buddha and Mahavira thinkers. They are not thinkers. They are enlightened beings. There is a difference of heaven and earth between a thinker and an enlightened being. They know, they do not think. Only someone who does not know is obsessed with thoughts.

I am sitting here now, and when the meeting is over, we will all stand up and walk out through the door. No one will think about where the door is because we can see the door. If a blind man is sitting here, as the meeting comes to an end, he will start thinking about where to go out. He will start thinking, "Where is the door? Where is the wall?" The person who can see does not think. Only the one who cannot see, thinks. Thinking is a sign of ignorance; it is not a sign of knowledge. Be aware that the more thinking you do, the more ignorant you are. When knowing happens, thinking will disappear, and emptiness will come into being.

I have said you should observe thoughts and allow them to be reduced to nothing, to become empty. Thoughts will disappear once you have become aware. Thoughts disappear through witnessing; when thoughts disappear, your intelligence is free. When a free intelligence comes upon the truth, it does not bother about knowing scriptures or doctrines. A free intelligence lets go of the shore and enters the limitless sea.

A small story, and then I will end my talk.

One evening a group of friends were out to have some fun. It was a beautiful full-moon night and they had drunk a lot. It was a beautiful night, so they all decided to go to the lake and take a boat trip. They sat down in a boat, picked up the oars and started to row. They continued to row until the last hour of the night. By dawn, when a cool breeze started to blow and touch their faces, and the moon had almost disappeared from the horizon, they had become a little sober. A couple of them became sober and said, "Friends, we must have come very far. We have been rowing the whole night; now it is time to go back. By the time we reach home it will be midday. We must be far from the shore." They thought, "Let us see how far we have come."

They were stunned at what they saw. They had not gone anywhere; the boat was in exactly the same place. They had forgotten to untie the chains, and so the boat was still in the same place. The chains were still tied to the boat. They were very surprised; they had rowed a great deal, but hadn't gone anywhere. They said, "We just wasted our effort in rowing the whole night and thinking we had gone a long way. We are in the same place."

Someone who wants to free his thinking and intelligence must inevitably untie his chains from the shore of belief. Someone who is tied somewhere to a belief must remember that he can't set off on a journey in the world of truth. He will not reach anywhere. At the end of his life he will find he is standing exactly where he started; he is standing exactly at the point where he was given the belief by his parents. The journey has been futile; the rowing has been futile. The effort has been wasted. At the time of death he is still bound by the same thoughts and beliefs that his parents and society gave him. The life of such a man has been a misfortune. His journey has been wasted. He forgot to untie his chains from the shore.

Untie your chains from the shore. Remove the chains from everything that society or anyone else has given you. Let your intelligence be liberated. Only a free intelligence allows you to fly and reach godliness; inhibiting thoughts and beliefs are hindrances for reaching the divine. We are all tied by chains.

The whole world is tied with chains. We cannot experience godliness because we are bound by those chains. Have courage and drop those chains, and see where your boat goes.

I will end my talk by quoting a statement of Ramakrishna. Ramakrishna said, "Release your boat, open the sails of your boat; the winds of existence are always ready to take you into the vast beyond."

Blessed are those who release their boats and open their sails. Unfortunate are the people who keep their boats tied to something and make an effort, only to meet with failure at the end.

Finally, I pray that existence may give you the strength and courage to release your boat from the shore of belief, so you can enter the endless sea of knowing. Existence is with those who have courage. What can even existence do for those who are weak and never start the journey?

Enough for today. Please accept my thanks. I am very grateful to you for listening to me with so much love. Please accept my greetings to the godliness within you.

2
Simplicity of Mind

Last night I told you a few things about freedom. I said the first condition for a man seeking truth is that his consciousness needs to be free: there is no mental slavery or bondage, his mind is not tied to any predetermined way or thought, his mind is not burdened or restricted in any way, and there is no limiting frame on his mind. Certainly a man who is not free cannot attain the truth. Mental slavery is very deep-rooted. I am not talking of the slavery that is political, social, or economical; I am talking of the slavery that is psychological. The person who is a slave psychologically may attain anything else, but he cannot experience the bliss and the blessedness and the light of life. That is what I talked about yesterday.

So, the first essential prerequisite is freedom of consciousness. This morning I will be talking about another prerequisite: simplicity of mind. The first prerequisite is the freedom of consciousness, the second is simplicity of mind.

If our minds are complicated, if our minds are entangled in conflicts, we are also not capable of knowing the truth. Our minds are not at all simple; our minds are very complicated, very chaotic, very entangled, filled with conflicts and paradoxes. And it is these complicated minds that hinder us.

How can someone who is complicated inside – entangled with thoughts and conflicts – open his eyes to any other reality? How can someone who is tremendously occupied inwardly and has inner conflicts, orient himself toward the truth? How can someone who fights with himself and is fragmented inside know the indivisible?

We are all fragmented. We are divided into many inner fragments, and all these fragments are fighting with one another.

Once it happened…

Christ went to a village and a young man went to meet him. Christ asked the young man, "What is your name? Before I talk to you about anything I would like to know your name."

The young man replied, "My name is Legion. I have a thousand names, which name should I tell you?"

Christ said, "At least you have told me the truth about yourself. Others mention a name, but inside them there are thousands of personalities."

Every person has many people inside him – you are a crowd. There is no individual inside you. You are not an individual; there is a crowd stuffed inside you. Mahavira said that man is polypsychic. Generally we think we have only one mind. Mahavira says we are polypsychic. Modern research also says that we are polypsychic. We have many minds in us at the same time.

If you think about it, you will realize you have many minds. When you are filled with anger, do you have the same mind as when you repent later on? The mind that repents is totally different. The mind that gives vent to anger is a different mind. You continue to repent, and you continue to be angry as well.

The voice of the mind that repents never reaches the mind that is angry. Otherwise the anger would have stopped.

You make the same mistake a thousand times. After making the mistake you repent, you are unhappy, and you decide you will never be angry again. If you were one individual, with only one mind inside you, the decision would be total. But you have many minds inside. The mind that decides is a different mind than the mind that acts. All your decisions remain just decisions, and your life goes on as before. Before going to sleep at night, you decide to get up at four o'clock the next day. You make up your mind to get up at four. But at four, someone inside you says to stay in bed – "What is the use? It is cold" – and you go back to sleep. In the morning when you get up, you start to repent and you think, "How did that happen? I had made up mind that I would get up at four, and I didn't get up. Tomorrow I will definitely get up." The next day, once again you find someone inside telling you, "What is the use of getting up so early? It is very cold, keep on sleeping." Is this mind the same one that took the decision? Or is it another mind?

Your mind has many parts. It is fragmented; it has many fragments. Because of these fragments, complications arise in you. Someone whose mind is not integrated is bound to be complicated. Moreover, the complications become multiplied because each mind is against the other minds.

Just think a little. You made all this conflict with your own hands. Education and conditioning have fragmented your mind. Its indivisibility has been destroyed. It is not integrated. You say you are only one person because you have only one name, one label; everyone knows you are one person. Search inside yourself, and you will find many people there. You will hear many voices inside you, voices that are different from you, voices that are against you. Have you ever thought about that?

Many times someone will say, "I did that in spite of myself." In spite of himself! A man kills someone in anger and later on he says, "I killed him in spite of myself." What kind of mad talk is that? How can someone kill in spite of himself if the opposite is not also inside him?

You must have felt many times, "When I was angry, I was not there at all." You must have felt many times, "When I became filled with sexual desire, I was not there; I do not know what happened to me." When you are angry, are you the same person as when you are peaceful? When you love, are you the same person as when you hate? No, you are not. Your face changes, something changes inside you. You have a multitude of minds, with many fragments inside you. A certain fragment takes possession of you, and you do something. After that part goes away, just like when the wheel of a cart turns – one spoke comes up and another goes down, the spokes keep changing, they keep changing their position – your mind changes. It has many minds within it. One mind comes up, and another mind goes down, and that produces complexity.

Only someone who has only one mind can be simple. Someone who has many minds is bound to be complex. And, each one of those minds is unaware of the others. The person himself knows that, because all his decisions remain incomplete. The mind that decides is not there when the decision has to be implemented.

You must have decided many times to speak the truth, and when the time comes, you find yourself telling a lie. You must have decided many times to love everyone, and when the time comes, you find yourself full of hatred. You must have decided many times that everyone would be your friend, but you realize that you seem to have many enemies. Since it is you who decides – you take the decision – from where does the opposite come? The opposite is already present within you. For the person you respect, you feel disrespect also in your mind. You have the opposite in you at the same time.

You see lovers constantly fighting with one another. They love, and they also fight with one another; they also hate one another. You see it with friends and with students. What one part of the mind does, another part of the mind always opposes. That is why love turns into hatred after a short while.

I was talking about this in Delhi recently. Someone said that the person we love, we love; we don't hate them. He asked, "How can you say such a thing?"

I told him, "Suppose you love your wife, and tomorrow you come to know she loves someone else. What will happen then? That very moment your love will turn into hatred. Can love ever turn into hatred? It is impossible. Actually, the hatred is hidden inside you. Love is on the surface, and the hatred is underneath. When the reason for love goes, the love goes, and the hatred comes to the surface."

There was a woman mystic whose name was Rabiya. She was a unique woman mystic. In the Koran she read the statement, "Hate the Devil," and she erased it. Hassan was a travelling mystic of those days, and once he was a guest at her home. In the early morning he wanted to read the Koran. So she gave him her Koran and he saw that one line had been erased.

To make an amendment in a religious scripture? To change a holy statement! He asked, "Who is the idiot who made a change in the holy Koran?"

Rabiya replied, "I had to do it."

"Why? Why did you do it? The scripture has been desecrated."

Rabiya replied, "I had a very big problem. In this scripture, it says, 'Hate the Devil.' I searched everywhere inside myself, and there was no hatred. If the Devil were to come in front of me, how would I hate him? After all, to hate someone you need to have hatred inside. Otherwise, where will it come from? If you put your bucket in a well that does not have any water in it, where will the water come from? It will only come if it is there." Rabiya said, "I have no more hatred inside me, there is only love. Whether it is God or the Devil; if both were to come and stand in front of me, I would be helpless. I can only love. I would give equal love to both. I do not have any hatred inside. I searched a great deal; I did not find any hatred inside."

If you search inside your love, you will find hatred. It is standing right behind the love; it is like a shadow of the love. For the person who is your friend, you have a feeling of hatred also in your mind. For the person you respect, you have a feeling of disrespect also in your mind. For the man you praise, the tendency to criticize him is also right behind. If these opposite tendencies are always present, how can your mind be simple? And how can a mind that is not simple know the truth?

Simplicity is essential. Simplicity is the most essential condition to attain godliness. It is necessary to understand our minds, which are complex. It is necessary to understand the opposite parts of our minds, their complexity, why they have become fragmented, and why they are divided into many parts. Unless we become indivisible, none of our prayers, none of our meditations, none of our yoga, no worship of ours will be worthwhile; everything will be useless. We may go to any temple, and we may go to any mosque and bow down to any god; there will be no meaning. Without becoming indivisible, there is no meaning. When we bow down our heads in front of a statue in a temple, inside there is distrust together with the trust; there is disrespect together with the respect; there is doubt together with the faith.

I used to visit my village. An old teacher of mine lived there; I visited him often. The last time I spent about a week in the village, and I went to his house every day. I would go there in the early morning. One day he sent me a message not to come. I asked his son why he had sent the message. The son said, "My father also asked me to give you this letter."

In the letter he had written, "I feel very happy when you come to see me. My joy knows no bounds when you come to my house. But I don't want you to come because yesterday when I sat down to worship, what you said to me crossed my mind. And I started to wonder whether what I was doing was foolish. Wasn't all this praying very childish? The stone statue lying in front of me, was it not just a piece of stone? I have been praying for thirty or forty years, and now I have started to have doubts in my mind. I became afraid. So I pray you, please do not come to my house again."

I wrote to him, saying that whether I came or not, what needed to happen, had happened. In all humbleness I wanted to tell him that I did not produce the doubt in his mind. He had been worshipping constantly for the last forty years, but the doubt had always been hiding behind.

Has doubt ever been erased by faith? You impose faith from the outside; doubt remains hiding on the inside. Has hatred ever been destroyed by love? You show love on your face, but hatred remains inside. Does the feeling of disrespect go away by showing respect? You impose respect from the outside, and inside the disrespect remains. You become more and more complex.

That is why I say you should give up any faith that has doubt behind it. When doubt disappears, what remains is called trust. A love that has hate hidden in it, I call useless. The day that hate goes, what is left is love. A friendship in which there is a possibility of enmity has no meaning. The day the feeling of enmity falls away, what is left is a feeling of friendship. In the same way, the happiness that has unhappiness hidden behind has no value. The day the suffering ends, what remains is bliss.

We are always full of opposites. The mind of a man who is full of opposites is complex. The mind of a man who is full of opposites will always be dual and in conflict.

It is important to understand that a mind that is always in conflict loses its capacity to know. If a person is always engaged in conflict, his consciousness, his awareness becomes duller and dimmer. A person who continually fights becomes insensitive because of the constant conflict. His sensitivity becomes less. A person who is always in conflict slowly, slowly becomes more dull. His intellect does not grow; it becomes weaker and weaker.

This is the reason we see that the brain of an old man, instead of becoming sharper, becomes weaker than that of a child. A body can become old, but there is no reason for a mind to age if it is not in conflict. If a mind is not in conflict, if a mind is not complex, if it is not divided and fragmented, if it is not filled with contradictions, there is no reason for it to become old. A mind becomes old due to constant conflict, constant fighting, always being full of contradictions. It is natural that the capability and sensitivity of someone who is always in conflict degenerates.

We grow old in the mind as well, although there is no reason for the mind to grow old. This conflict of ours, this struggle, this fragmentation of the mind, is only because of ourselves. We are the ones who divide it into fragments. Due to our own ignorance, we break ourselves up into fragments. We need to try and understand how we break up the mind; only then can we understand what simplicity is, and how simplicity of mind can arise.

Before I go into it deeply, I would like to tell you that generally when we say someone is very simple, or when it is said we should be simple, that is not the kind of simplicity I am talking about. We are generally told that we should be simple. I am not talking about that kind of simplicity. Behind that kind of simplicity, complexity is always hidden. A man can pretend to be simple. A man can make a show of being simple in many ways. He may not wear fashionable clothes, and start to wear clothes made from coarse fabric. We say he is a very simple man. He can go even further and wear only a loincloth. We say he is very simple. He might go even further and be naked. We talk about what a simple man he is. That is not simplicity. Instead of eating two meals a day, a man can start to eat only one meal a day. We say what a simple man he is; he eats only once a day. If a man does not eat meat, if he is a vegetarian, we say what a simple man he is; or if a man does not smoke, does not drink, does not play cards, we say what a simple man he is.

No one becomes simple so easily. That is not the underlying basis of simplicity. On the contrary, such people are very complicated. That type of man shows simplicity on the outside, but his inner complexity is not destroyed; it remains there.

Once I was travelling by train, and a monk was in my compartment. We were the only two passengers in the compartment. A lot of people had gathered to say good-bye and see him off at the station. He certainly had a big following. He had wrapped a single piece of sacking around himself, which he had tied with a rope. Just a piece of sacking, tied with a piece of rope. His luggage was just a small bamboo basket, in which he was carrying two or three more pieces of sacking and two or three pieces of rope. That was his only luggage.

After his friends departed, he picked up his basket and started counting the number of cloths in it. Only I was in the compartment with him. I kept on observing him silently. He counted the number of pieces, and found they were exactly the same as before. Then he put them back in the basket. In the night he fell asleep. He asked me when the train would be arriving at the station where he had to get off. I said that it would arrive around six in the morning and to sleep with no worries, because our compartment was going to be detached from the train at that station. There was no reason to worry, he could sleep soundly.

Nevertheless, I noticed that he stood up at midnight and again asked someone else the same thing, when the train would arrive at his station. The train had stopped at some other station, and he asked someone if it had passed his station. I said to him, "Look, you cannot miss that station. This compartment is going to be detached there. So you should not worry at all; go back to sleep. Why are you so worried?" On the outside he was wearing only a piece of cloth, and on the inside he had so much anxiety and useless worry.

In the morning when I woke up, I observed him adjusting his cloth and tying it more tightly. It did not seem to be correct to him. Then he took the cloth off and tied it around in another way. He repeated the same action a third time. That too he did not find to be right. He got up and stood in front of the mirror to see whether he had tied it in the right way or not.

How can I call that simplicity? It is complexity. That man was even more complicated than a man who wears expensive clothes. The pretense of simplicity on the outside does not have any meaning. It is not simplicity at all. Simplicity is a very different thing.

It is just like someone who puts paper flowers in his house. There is a great difference between paper flowers and real flowers. Simplicity cannot be cultivated; it cannot be imposed from the outside. If the mind inside is indivisible, simplicity starts to radiate by itself. Then what a man wears makes no difference, what he eats makes no difference, how he sits down and walks makes no difference. All this becomes simple by itself. If the mind inside is integrated, simplicity enters the outer layer of life by itself. If the mind inside is fragmented, no matter how much outer simplicity someone imposes on himself, it will not be simplicity. It will be cultivated and has no value. It has been cultivated from the outside. Can simplicity that has been cultivated from the outside have any value? Such simplicity is cultivated; it is not spontaneous.

Kabir has said, "Seekers, spontaneous enlightenment is right. That which is born naturally and evolves naturally is the best. That which is unnatural, imposed, and practiced is useless."

Once I happened to be in a village. I had a friend who was a monk. He was getting ready to be a naked monk. When I approached his hut, I saw that he was walking naked in his hut; I could see him through the window. When I knocked on the door and he opened it, he had wrapped a cloth around himself. I said, "When I saw you through the window you were walking naked in your hut. Why are you wearing clothes now?"

He said, "I was practicing to be naked. Sooner or later I will have to be a naked monk, so I was practicing for that. First I will practice to be naked alone. Then I will practice it among friends. Then I will go out of the house a little way, then in the village and finally out in the town. In that way slowly, slowly I will get used to it."

I told him, "You should join a circus. There is no need for you to be a monk. You should join a circus."

This is why I tell you that the nakedness cultivated through practice is not the nakedness that must have happened to Mahavira. His nakedness did not come through practice; it came through innocence. His nakedness was not practiced. His consciousness had become so simple and innocent that clothes had become unnecessary, and they were dropped. The clothes were not renounced, they fell away. A nakedness that happens like that is meaningful. Nakedness that happens by renouncing clothes and is cultivated by practice can be done by anyone in a circus. That is not difficult at all, but it is not the point.

For instance, it is understandable that a man is so filled with the memory of the divine that he forgets to eat; the day goes by and fasting happens naturally. I cannot understand that a man would remain hungry the whole day through effort and practice. Fasting means to be near the divine, to be close to it, intimate with it. It is understandable that one's consciousness is so intimate with existence that one forgets to eat, and fasting occurs spontaneously. In the other case, a fast that has been practiced is totally useless; it does not have any value.

Everything that is practiced is useless. Only what comes naturally is meaningful. What is practiced does not have any meaning. Whatever is significant in life happens; it is not practiced.

If I practice love for you, will that love be true? How can a love that has been practiced be true? A practiced love will be acting, it will be hypocrisy. A loves that arises, a love that starts to spring up within me, its blocked gates opening and the current of love starting to flow from within, is understandable. If I make an effort, try hard to love you, what will be the value of that love? In the same way, simplicity that has been practiced has no value.

We can see people all around us practicing simplicity. Those we call monks have practiced simplicity; they have put in all their effort. For every small thing they have a rule and a structure – when to get up, when to go to sleep, what to eat, what to wear. A monk has to keep an account of each and every thing. There is a lot of planning. It would have been better if he had been an engineer; it would have been better if he had been the manager of some company; it would have been better if he had been operating machines somewhere – his brain would have proved to be very competent in handling machines – but he is a monk.

The life of a real monk is spontaneous. The life of a real monk is not practiced, it is spontaneous. What takes place within him happens spontaneously.

In Japan there was an emperor. He told his ministers he would like to meet a monk. His prime minister said, "A monk? You can find monks in every nook and corner of this country. You can go anywhere and meet them."

In Japan there are many monks – in Buddhist countries there are a great number of monks. In Cambodia the population of the country is about six million, and there are about six hundred thousand monks. It is the same in Japan; there are many monks. The same is the case in Sri Lanka.

His ministers told the emperor, "There is no shortage of monks or holy people here. If you wish we can gather a big crowd of monks."

The emperor said, "No, I want to come face-to-face with a monk."

They asked, "What do you mean by coming face-to-face with a monk? Just go on any road and you will find plenty of monks."

The emperor said, "If they were monks, I would not have asked you for a meeting. They all appear to be actors to me. Does someone become a monk by wearing a special type of robe, having his hair shaved in a special way, and carrying a certain kind of bag on his shoulder? They all appear very immature to me. Inside, they are talented actors. They could all be actors, but in what way are they monks?"

You should go and see monks. Someone has a special type of mark on his forehead; another wears a special type of clothes; another has some other peculiar thing. Their followers do exactly the same thing. All that seems to be very childish and immature. Can any intelligent and thoughtful person ever do something like that?

Once a sannyasin went to Gandhi and told him he would like to serve people in some way. Gandhi looked at him from head to toe and said, "Before you can do any social service, you will have to give up those saffron robes."

He asked, "Why? How are they a hindrance?"

Gandhi said, "The very fact that you are wearing those robes means you want people to think you are a sannyasin. Otherwise there is no reason for wearing those robes. You are a sannyasin, so you can be a sannyasin in any clothes. People will not think you are a sannyasin in any other robes, only in those. You want people to think you are a sannyasin, and the man who wants people to think that he is a sannyasin is not a sannyasin. What has sannyas got to do with what people think?"

The emperor said, "I want to meet a monk."

The ministers searched to find out if such a monk really existed. With great difficulty they learned that a man like that did exist, and he lived in a hut just outside the village. Some people said he was a monk.

The emperor went there. He arrived early in the morning. He thought the monk must get out of bed early in the morning, so he arrived early. It was around seven or seven-thirty in the morning. The sun had risen, but the monk was fast asleep. There was a statue of Buddha and the monk was resting his feet on it. He was still fast asleep.

The emperor asked, "What type of monk is this? He puts his feet on the statue of Buddha and he sleeps so late!"

The people who brought him there told the emperor, "You should not be so hasty in reaching a decision. It is not that easy to recognize a monk."

It is because we are so quick to make up our minds that so many pseudo-monks appear to be monks. Anyone can get up at four; is that a very difficult thing to do? Anyone can sit with folded hands in front of a statue of Buddha; is that very difficult?

"You should not be so quick to take a decision. This man is something special. A man who puts his feet on a statue of Buddha is not an ordinary man. Only a real monk can rest his feet on Buddha, no one else can do it. Wait a little longer, do not be in a hurry to reach a conclusion."

The monk got up around eight o'clock. The moment he opened his eyes the emperor asked him, "Why are you getting up so late? A monk should get up early in the morning."

The monk replied, "Yes, I always get up at the most auspicious time of the morning. Whenever I get up, for me that is the most auspicious hour of the day. When existence wakes me, I get up; when existence puts me to sleep, I go to sleep. Neither do I decide from my side when to get up, nor do I decide from my side when to sleep. I left myself in the hands of existence the day I became a monk. That day I left myself in the hands of existence; now whatever happens, happens. When I sit in the sun and the sun becomes very hot, existence says, now go into the shade, and I go into the shade. When the shade becomes cold and existence says, go into the sun, I go into the sun. I have left myself in the hands of existence. Now I am only breathing, I am no longer myself. As a result, when sleep is over and my eyes open, I get up; when I feel hungry, I beg for food."

The emperor said, "I am very surprised. Don't you have any rules or structures? No structure at all?"

The monk replied, "That is all there is to it. No rules, no structure. For the person who leaves himself in the hands of existence, there are no rules or structures."

All rules and structures come from the ego. All the systems of rules and methods come from the ego. People want to impose something on life, and all rules arise from that. The man who wants to impose something on life, the man who expects something special from life, that it should be like this and not like that, the man who condemns one thing and accepts another, cannot be simple. Simplicity is the first essential condition for a real monk. The essential condition for attaining truth is simplicity.

The monk said that a man who is like the moisture in the air and goes wherever the winds take him, who is like a dry leaf that falls wherever the winds make it fall and rises again wherever the winds cause it to rise... Only a man who is like a dry leaf can be simple, everyone else is bound to be complex. A man who is like a piece of wood floating on the surface of the sea, who goes wherever the waves take him and lands wherever the winds land him, who does not have any structured wish of his own about what should be done and what should not be done, who does not project anything on life – only such a man can be simple.

How can someone who has rules and regulations for all twenty-four hours of the day be simple? How can someone who tries to mold himself in a special way around the clock be simple? Anyone who makes an effort to cultivate himself cannot be simple. A man who tries to attain godliness and makes an effort to be a monk, a man who forces himself to be honorable, a man who is always busy being nonviolent, being truthful, not being angry – how can a man who makes all that effort be simple? Such a man cannot be simple. A man who sacrifices himself for an ideal can never be simple – and every man surrenders himself to some ideal or other.

Mahavira lived two thousand, five hundred years ago, Christ lived two thousand years ago, Buddha lived two thousand, five hundred years ago, and Rama lived much, much earlier than all of them. Krishna also lived a long time ago. Yet we cling to their ideals. The followers of Buddha have been trying to become like Buddha for the last two thousand, five hundred years. Has any other man become Buddha? No one has succeeded in imitating Buddha in the last two thousand, five hundred years. Has any other man become Mahavira? In the last two thousand, five hundred years, no one has been able to do it. Has anyone else become Christ? Two thousand years of experience contradicts it. Even so, millions of people are trying to become Christ; millions are trying to become Buddha, and millions are trying to become Mahavira. There must be some fundamental mistake in that way of being.

Someone who tries to be like someone else becomes complex. Naturally, he has to become complex. He starts to deny who he is and to impose the other person on himself. He starts to deny his reality and to assume the ideals of the other person. He becomes complicated, he becomes complex. His mind is fragmented; he breaks apart inside. Conflict is born within him. The biggest problem is that in order to become Mahavira, it is essential to be simple; to become Buddha, it is essential to be simple; to become Christ, it is essential to be simple – and because of the imitation, those who try to follow them are complicated.

Look at the situation. No one can be simple by copying another person. Imitating someone else means you try to be like someone else without understanding the person you are, who you are. Without understanding who you are, you are trying to be like another person. You leave aside who you are, and you start to wear the covering of the other person. You force yourself to act, to be a hypocrite.

A so-called religious country is full of hypocrisy, as our country is. It is difficult to find a more hypocritical country than ours. It is difficult to find a more complicated country, a more complicated race, a more complicated creed than we are. No other race has as much hypocrisy as we have inside us. The only reason for it is that we are all involved in the mad race of following someone, some ideal, without understanding who we are – whereas any real revolution in life starts by understanding who we actually are. It starts by understanding exactly who we are.

One person is angry, someone else is very greedy, still someone else is very arrogant. If an arrogant man tries to become humble, what will happen? If someone is egoistic and all his education, culture, and preachers tell him to drop his ego and become very peaceful, and he tries to give up his ego, what will he do? Can he give up the ego? Can he drop the ego? Who will drop the ego? The one who tries to drop the ego is the very ego itself.

When he feels he is giving up the ego, the man will say, "I have given up the ego; I have become humble. I am feeling humble and I have no arrogance in me." What is all that? All that is just part of arrogance itself. Can an ego ever drop the ego? In the dropping, it will become stronger, it will become more subtle.

That is why the sannyasin's ego is much more subtle than the ordinary man's ego. It has to be. Ordinary people mingle with one another. Sannyasins never mingle with one another. If you tell sannyasins to mingle with one another, they cannot.

Once I told a famous monk that he should go and meet a certain monk. He said it would be a little difficult. What was the difficulty? The problem was that if two monks were to meet, who would bow down in greeting first? Who would sit where? Who would have the higher seat, and who would sit on the lower seat?

Once I went to attend a religious festival. About thirty or forty monks belonging to various faiths had also been invited. The organizer of the festival wanted all the invitees to sit on the same platform, but they could not, because one was a *shankaracharya*, a head priest of the Hindus. He wanted to sit on a throne, and that was the only place he would sit.

And when a *shankaracharya* sat on a throne, how could the other monks agree to sit at his feet? They said they also wanted to sit on thrones. Then there was the worry about whose throne would be higher and whose throne would be lower.

Do you think those people were saints, or were they mad? Is that humility or the ultimate peak of ego? It is a refined form of ego. So-called holy people fight with one another, and they make ordinary people also fight with one another; wherever the ego is, it will create conflict, clash, and fighting.

That is arrogance. The ego can never give up the ego. When it is involved in giving up the ego, it is the ego itself that thinks, "I should be humble." So what will it do? It will make a pretense of being humble. When an egoistic man meets you, he will bow his head and tell you he is nothing. When he says he is nothing, inside he knows he is something. When he says he is nothing… Only a man who knows inside that he is something says that he is nothing. Otherwise he doesn't say it. How can a greedy man drop greed? If he gives up greed, it is only because of greed that he gives it up.

Once, I heard a monk explaining to an assembly, "If you give up greed, you will be peaceful; if you give up greed, you will be doing a good deed; if you give up greed, you will obtain moksha, liberation."

I told the monk that only a very greedy man would agree with him, because only a man who is greedy for moksha would think about giving up greed. When a man who is greedy for peace thinks about dropping greed, it is a function of greed itself, an extension of greed. How can a greedy man drop greed?

Actually, nothing evil can ever be given up. It is like when there is darkness; darkness itself cannot be removed. If this building is filled with darkness, we cannot remove it by pushing it away. If someone tries to push away darkness, what do we call him? We call him mad. His brain is not right. Can anyone push away darkness? Yes, one can light a lamp. When there is light, the darkness disappears by itself; it is nowhere to be found.

In the same way, the ego cannot be removed. When simplicity arises, the ego can no longer be found. Greed itself cannot be removed. When peace arises, greed can no longer be found. In life, evil cannot be given up. When good is awakened, when the divine is awakened, darkness goes away by itself.

If we are involved in giving up the ego, life becomes complex – and we are all involved in giving up the ego. I meet people who tell me they have to drop the violence inside them. I ask them, "How can you drop violence?" Yes, love can be awakened, but violence cannot be dropped. People say they have to drop being false. Truth can be awakened, but being false cannot be dropped. When we become involved in the language of giving up, complications begin, conflict begins.

Our minds are filled with so many conflicts. We want to give up so many things. But giving up is not the nature of life; it is attaining that is the principle of life. If we attain something higher, the lower goes away by itself. If we attain the higher, the lower disappears. If the superior is attained, the inferior disappears. If the superior is attained, the inferior makes place for it. If light comes, darkness leaves.

However, darkness cannot leave the place by itself. The arrival of light is primary, and the disappearance of the lower is secondary. The arrival, the coming of real simplicity that causes the complex to disappear, cannot be imposed. It has to be awakened from inside. What is the principle to awaken it inside? The principle is that you should first of all free yourself from all ideals. Ideals make you complex.

Before you try to make yourself into something, you should try to know what you are. You ask who you should be like. I am saying, that is meaningless: you should know what you are like. It is logical that you should know what you are like. If you know the full reality about yourself, with that knowledge, transformation will begin. If a man knows his anger fully, the anger will disappear. You don't need to do anything else to make anger disappear, you only need to know the anger – but you have never known your anger.

You say, "I have been angry many times." I tell you, I have been all over the country, and I am still searching for a man who has known his anger. You have never known your anger. When you are angry, you are not present. You are unconscious, you are not in your senses. Can a man ever be angry if he is present? Anger cannot happen if you are present. If you are present, anger is impossible. If your presence is total at that moment, if you are alert and aware when the tendency to be angry is there in your mind, anger will be impossible. Anger cannot be discharged. Whenever you are aware, whatever is wrong becomes impossible. For evil to happen, you must be unconscious. If a man who wants to do something evil is intoxicated, the evil deed is even easier, because in intoxication, awareness fades away.

All religions are against intoxicants because of only one thing. Otherwise there is nothing wrong with intoxicants.

What is wrong in drinking alcohol? There is nothing bad in alcohol, the only thing is that when you are intoxicated, your awareness disappears; you become even more unconscious. All sins come from unconsciousness. The more unconscious you are, the more sins you commit.

When you are angry, you are unconscious. When you are tormented by lust, you are unconscious. You are not in your senses. You are not your own self. Something is pulling you, and you are not in your senses at all; you don't know where you are going. Just observe a man in anger. Look at a man who has been gripped by lust. Look at his face, observe his emotions. Look at his body. You will find that he is unconscious. When you are angry, not only are you unconscious at the level of the mind, but also at the level of the body. Scientists say your glands start to release poison, and under the influence of that poison you are almost in a state of intoxication. You almost reach a state of intoxication. You are unconscious both at the level of the body and at the level of the mind.

Buddha had a disciple. He was newly initiated into the path of seekers that Buddha called sannyas. He asked Buddha, "Where shall I go to beg for alms today?"

Buddha replied, "There is a disciple of mine; you can go to her."

He went there. When he sat down to take his meal, he was shocked to see that the meal served to him was exactly the one he was thinking about on the way to the woman's house. He had always loved that dish, and during his walk he wondered who would give him exactly the food he loved: "Who will give me my favorite food today?" He had been a prince just before, and he was used to eating what he liked. Still, he was surprised to see the same food served for him at his hostess' house. He thought it must be a coincidence that the same food was cooked on that day.

While eating he thought, "I used to rest after my meal every day. Today I am a beggar and have to leave after my lunch. I will have to walk two or three miles under the hot sun."

While he was eating, the woman was fanning him, and then she said, "Brother, I would be very obliged if you would take a rest in my house after you have eaten your meal."

The monk was again very surprised and thought, "Does my thought reach her somehow?" Again he thought, "It must be a coincidence that she made the request just at the moment I was thinking about it."

A mat was laid out for him and he lay down. As he lay down it occurred to him, "Today, I have neither my own bed nor my own shelter. I have nothing."

The hostess, who was on her way out, suddenly stopped and returned. She said, "Brother, this bed is neither yours nor mine, even this home does not really belong to anyone. Please do not worry."

Now it was difficult for him to believe all this was just a coincidence. He sat up and asked, "I am very surprised; can you sense my feelings?"

The hostess started to laugh. She said, "The mind calms down after experimenting with meditation for a while. Then you can sense other people's feelings a little bit."

He got up at once. He felt totally embarrassed and started to shiver. The hostess asked, "Why are you embarrassed? Why are you shivering? Please rest. Just lay down."

The monk said, "Please allow me to leave." He lowered his eyes and took off like a thief.

The hostess asked, "What is the matter? Why are you disturbed?"

He did not even look back. He went straight to Buddha and said, "I can never go to that door again."

Buddha asked, "What happened? Wasn't the food good? Didn't she show respect to you? Did she do something wrong?"

He replied, "The food was exactly what I love to eat. I received great respect. But I will not go there anymore. Please do not ask me to go there again."

Buddha asked, "Why are you so embarrassed? Why are you so disturbed?"

He replied, "That hostess can read others' thoughts. While I was taking my meal, sensual thoughts also arose in my mind at the sight of that beautiful woman. She must have sensed those thoughts too. With what kind of face can I go to her house? I just lowered my eyes and escaped. She addressed me as brother, venerable sir and so on. She paid respect to me. I was shaken to my very roots. She must have sensed what arose in my mind. Still she addressed me as venerable sir and paid respect to me. Please forgive me; I will not go there," he insisted.

Buddha said, "I sent you to her knowingly. It is part of your meditation. You have to go there. You will go there every day. You must go there until you come to me and say you can go there every day without any problem. Until then you have to go there. It is part of your meditation."

He asked, "How can I go there? How can I go there with dignity? If similar thoughts arise in me in the coming days, what am I supposed to do?"

Buddha said to him, "Just do one thing, a small experiment. You do not need to do anything else. Observe each and every thought that arises in you, go there and keep watching the thoughts. If sensuality arises, observe that too. If feelings take place, sensuality arises, anger arises, keep watching whatever appears, and do not do anything else. Remain aware. Just like when someone lights a candle in a dark house, and everything in the house becomes visible, keep your consciousness awake so that whatever is happening within you is observed. Everything is watched with absolute clarity. Go there in this manner."

The monk went. He had to go. He was afraid; who knew what would happen? But he came back fearless, he came back dancing. He went there afraid, but returned with a dance. He went there with lowered eyes, but returned with his eyes looking up at the sky. He was almost flying when he returned. He fell at Buddha's feet and said, "Thank you. What happened? When I was aware, I found that there was silence. When I climbed the stairs of her house, I could even feel my breath going in and out. I could even hear my heart beat. There was so much silence in me. When a thought arose, I could observe it. I climbed the stairs of her house in absolute peace. While I climbed the steps, I knew that I was placing the right foot on the ground and raising the left foot. When I entered the house and sat down for lunch, for the first time in my life I could even observe each and every bite while I ate. I could even feel the vibrations of my hand. I could even feel the touch and experience the vibration of my breath. I was astonished that there was nothing inside me. There was absolute silence; there was no thought, no sensuality."

Buddha said, "When one is inwardly totally aware, inwardly totally awake, and full of consciousness, all disturbances disappear. It is just like when a lamp is lit, a thief does not come to the house. Thieves don't enter a house when a light is on. In the same way, when a mind is filled with awareness, with light, distortions stop coming. The mind becomes empty."

I tell you, you have never observed anger, because if you had watched anger, the anger would have disappeared. You have never observed sex; if you had watched it, it would have disappeared. Whatever is seen at the level of the mind disappears. Whatever is seen in its totality disappears. That which is left after the disappearance is love, true celibacy; it is non-anger, peace, nonviolence, and compassion. It is our self-nature. It does not have to be brought from anywhere. Only the outer elements that are covering it will disappear. That which is inside us will be manifested.

Godliness is our self-nature. In that self-nature, compassion is spontaneous, love is spontaneous, celibacy is spontaneous, kindness and nonviolence and truthfulness and nonattachment are spontaneous. If alien elements disappear, that spontaneity will manifest. That is why I have said that enlightenment is spontaneous and simple. The statement of Kabir that I quoted, "Seekers, spontaneous enlightenment is right," means that someone who watches spontaneously attains to enlightenment. His disturbances will disappear, and the truth will arise from within.

That will not happen by following anyone, it will happen by turning in, into your own self. It will not happen by following anyone, it will happen by following your own patterns of thought. You do not have to follow Mahavira and Buddha, you have to observe each movement of your anger and sex, you have to notice them and recognize them. There is no need for you to create any ideal. The supreme is present inside you. You do not have to become anything; if you can know who you are, everything will happen.

When we are involved in becoming something, complexity, entanglements, and conflict are born. Don't be involved in becoming anything; begin to know that which is. No need to be worried. Do not be afraid of anger; do not be afraid of sexuality; do not be afraid of jealousy; do not be afraid of hatred; do not be afraid of attachment; do not be afraid of greed. There is no need to feel afraid; enter these things. Bring awareness to them. Know them, recognize them with awareness. Observe them. Enter them.

The one who enters his greed reaches non-greed. The one who enters his anger reaches non-anger. The one who enters his sex has the experience of celibacy. We remain outside only out of fear and agitation, and we never enter them. We never wish to know them. We never make an effort to reach their innermost roots by entering them. We remain outside out of fear.

Evil people destroy themselves by doing bad things. Good people destroy themselves through the fear of doing bad things.

Once it happened…

An old man was sitting on the outskirts of his town. He was a mystic, and he lived outside the town. At night he saw a huge and fierce-looking shadow enter the town. It was just a shadow, and fiery-looking. He asked, "Who are you? Whose shadow is this and where is it going?"

He heard a voice saying, "I am a plague, and I have come to kill a thousand bad people in the town."

He asked, "Only bad people?"

"Only bad people," it replied and continued, "I will stay in the town for three days, and I will destroy a thousand bad people."

During those three days, many thousands died in that town. Among them were not only bad people, but good people, monks, and noblemen also. The old mystic waited for the shadow to come out of the town on the third day to ask it why it had deceived him.

When the shadow returned on the third day, the old mystic said, "Stop! Tell me why you deceived me, lied to me. You said earlier that you were going to destroy only a thousand bad people. During these three days thousands of people have been destroyed, and there were many good and decent people among them."

The plague replied, "I killed only a thousand bad people; the remaining good people died out of fear." It said, "I did not kill them; I killed only a thousand bad people, the remaining good people died out of fear. I am responsible for only a thousand people, the rest of them died by themselves."

Even though it is a completely fictitious story, it is true. Bad people die from anger, and good people die from the fear of anger.

There is a third way: it is neither a question of having anger nor a question of fighting with anger. It is a question of knowing anger. It is not a question of being angry, allowing the anger to lead you. Nor is it a question of forcing non-anger to be there, out of the fear of anger. It is a question of knowing anger and thus ending it. By knowing it, it disappears. By knowing, complexities disappear. There is no revolution greater than knowing.

While we were coming here, on the way someone asked, "If we have inner knowledge, what will we do? Once we have knowledge, what will be our behavior? If we achieve knowledge, how will we implement it in our daily life?" The very question is wrong. The very question is wrong. It would be as if someone would ask, "When there is light, what should we do with the darkness?" As if someone would ask, "The light has been turned on, but what should we do with the darkness?" What would we tell him?

We would tell him, "That means you have not understood the meaning of light." The very meaning of turning on the light is that there is no more darkness. Having inner knowledge means that there is no ignorance. When the ignorance is gone, the behavior that comes out of ignorance is not there. How can it be? Inner ignorance brings about bad conduct; inner knowledge brings about good conduct. Knowledge doesn't have to be brought into the behavior, just like when there is ignorance, bad conduct happens on its own.

Do you bring about anger? Have you ever brought about anger? You always find anger has come. Have you ever brought about anger? Have you ever brought about hatred? You always find it has come. What does "it has come" mean? If it comes, that means there is inner ignorance, and wrong behavior follows. In the same way, if there is inner knowledge, right behavior arises. It does not have to be cultivated. If there is inner knowledge, love will follow in the same way as hate comes now; compassion will follow in the same way as cruelty comes now; nonviolence will follow in the same way as violence comes now. Inner ignorance flows into wrong behavior. Inner knowledge flows into right behavior. Right behavior cannot be imposed; it springs, flows, and comes into being through inner knowledge.

Everything in life flows. Nothing is brought about. I have told you that there should be simplicity in life, that there should be no complexity in it. You should not take it to mean you have to bring about simplicity. It only means you have to know your complexity and enter it. The way to enter complexity is to be aware of the complexity and all the movements of the mind.

Yesterday I told you to be a witness of your thoughts, and freedom will follow. Be a witness of your feelings, and simplicity will follow. Someone who starts to know thought becomes free from thought. Someone who starts to know feelings becomes free from feelings. Knowing thought is freedom from thought; knowing feelings is freedom from feelings.

When our feelings are complex, we cannot know truth. If thoughts are complex, we cannot know truth. When thoughts are simple, if feelings are simple, an inner preparation takes place that opens our eyes so we can know truth. That is why I talked about the second step: simplicity of mind.

Tomorrow I will talk about the third step: emptiness of mind. There are only three steps: freedom of consciousness, simplicity of mind, and emptiness of mind. One who sharpens his freedom, simplicity, and emptiness, will attain enlightenment.

I am grateful that you listened to what I have said with love. I bow down to the godliness in all of you; please accept my greetings to the godliness within you.

3
The Real Answer Is Your Inner Perception

The first question:

Osho,
If all religious scriptures are hypocritical, what about the scriptures of the Vedas and the Upanishads? Should we believe them to be true or not?

You never read what is written in the scriptures. You read only what you can read, not what is in the scriptures. It is necessary to understand that.

When you read the Gita, or read the Upanishads, or the Bible, or some other scripture, do you think all the people who read it understand the same thing? Without question, there will be as many meanings taken away as there are people reading it. What you understand does not belong to the scripture; it comes from your own understanding. This is natural. You can understand only at your level of understanding, your conditioning, and your education.

When you understand the Gita, you should not think you have understood the statements of Krishna. You have understood only your own statements. Even though there might be some truth in the scripture, truth is not attained by understanding the scripture. Please understand this rightly. There might be some truth in the scripture, but truth is not known by understanding the scripture. Yes, if the truth has been attained, the scripture can be understood. Why?

Until you have attained the same state of consciousness in which Krishna made the statements, his statements cannot be understood. Whatever you understand will be only your own understanding. That is the reason why there is so much controversy about the scriptures. There are a thousand commentaries on the Gita. Either Krishna was mad, having a thousand meanings at the same time, or he had only one meaning. That there are thousands of interpretations implies that there are thousands of meanings. All those commentaries are definitely not about Krishna's Gita, rather they are information about the state of the authors' intellects. They are projections of their own thoughts. There cannot be a thousand meanings in Krishna's Gita. The truth is that there are as many meanings as there are people who read the Gita. You should not make the mistake of thinking that the meaning you understand in the Gita is the meaning of the Gita; it is your own meaning.

When you read a scripture, you do not attain truth, you only take the meaning from what you know already – and that is not the truth. If someone knows truth he can understand the scripture, but you cannot know truth by understanding the scripture. That is the reason that, although the religious books of all religions state the same truth, their followers always fight with one another, there is opposition between their believers. In this world, there are many sects in the name of truth. Truth is one and sects are many. Doesn't all this indicate that it is we who create sects, not truth? As thinking continues to grow in the world, there will be as many sects as there are people. Thinking gives birth to every individual's own opinion.

When I say that truth cannot be attained by reading the scriptures, you should understand what I mean. You can only understand as far as your state of consciousness, not more than that. By reading a scripture, you only obtain your own meaning, you do not know the meaning of the scripture. There may be truth in the scripture, but you will not attain the truth by studying the scripture.

That is why I said study is not the way to know truth; meditation is the way. Reading things and collecting them in your mind, which becomes memory, is not truth. Rather, when you attain the state of nothingness by dropping all thoughts – there are no thoughts in your consciousness – what you perceive in that state of silence is truth. Once you have experienced truth, the scriptures have no purpose. You know yourself what the scripture says.

I think what I am saying is now clear to you. I am speaking here; there is only one speaker and that is me. There is also only one purpose and one meaning in what I am saying. Do you think that you, the listener, are listening to exactly what is being said? If you are listening to exactly what is being said, and I asked what I have said, do you think all of you would have the same opinion? There would be many opinions. That means you have not all heard the same thing as I have said. You have all heard something different. You are bound to hear something different, because your thoughts and conditionings are so different that my statement has a totally different meaning when it reaches you. You will project that different meaning on me, saying I have said it.

In the same way you project your meaning on Krishna, on the Upanishads, on Christ. You project your meaning and you say they have said it. Never be under this illusion. Whatever you say, only you are saying it; you should not put the name of anyone else on it. If you are in a position to know truth, there is no need to read the scriptures. If you are not in a state to know the truth, nothing will happen by reading the scriptures.

That is why I said a man can continue to read the scriptures all his life. He can keep on reading as many scriptures as he wants to; nothing is going to happen. Yes, he will collect a lot of thoughts, and if he wants to give discourses, he can give discourses. His ego will be satisfied when he gives discourses; there is nothing more satisfying to the ego than giving discourses. The delight and enjoyment that a person receives by giving lectures to others is not found in anything else.

After reading the scriptures, you can preach. After reading the scriptures, you can produce other scriptures if you want, you can write other scriptures. That is possible, but you will never come face-to-face with the truth. For truth to be manifested you do not need a collection of thoughts; you will have to let go of all thoughts, make yourself empty of all thoughts. Truth is present inside you. Truth is present all around you, but you do not have the eyes to see it.

An incident is mentioned in the life of Buddha…

Once he went to a village, and some people brought a blind man to him. They said, "This man is our friend, and he cannot see. We tried to explain to him that light exists, that there is a sun, but he does not believe it. He refuses to believe. He does not accept it. Not only does he refuse to accept it, but he tries to convince us that we are wrong, that there is no such thing as light. He uses so much logic and reasoning that he invariably wins and we lose. When we heard you were coming to town, we thought we would take him to you so you could make him understand that light exists."

Buddha replied, "No, I will not make him understand anything. I can make you understand a few things."

The friends were very surprised. They said, "What do we need to understand? We tell him that light exists, then he says, 'If light exists, I would like to touch it and feel it. You can touch and feel everything that exists.'" We say, "Light exists and he says, 'If light exists I would like to hear its sound, hear its voice. If something exists, you can rub it against something else and produce a sound.' So we are helpless."

Buddha said, "The mistake is yours. It is madness to try to explain what light is to a man who is blind. Light cannot be explained, light has to be seen. You cannot think about light, you have to perceive light. You do not have to develop a conception of what light is; you only have to experience light. If you try to explain light to him knowing perfectly well he is blind, you are mad, and he is right in what says. It is better to take him to a doctor than to a thinker. He needs treatment, not reasoning. Don't try to make him understand; get his eyes treated. If he can see, he will come to know what light is without your telling him. If he is blind, no matter how much you try to make him understand, he can never know what light is."

They took him to a doctor for treatment. After a while, the film was removed from his eyes and he could see. Then he said to his friends, "I am sorry. Light exists, but I did not have the eyes to see. Whatever you told me was futile. Explaining to me through words something I had no experience of was futile. Your talking seemed useless to me, and I felt that all your talk of light was only to prove that I was blind. I thought you talked about light just in order to prove me blind. Now I know light exists because I have the eyes to see."

Truth is also something not to be thought about; it has to be directly perceived. Truth cannot be studied, it can only be experienced. For truth, you also have to open a kind of eye inside, only then can you perceive it, not by reading any scripture. You can teach a blind man as much as you want about light and explain it to him, but what will happen? He may also start to repeat what you say, but those words cannot open his eyes. They cannot make him have an experience. He cannot have direct perception.

For truth, eyes are also needed. Not thought, not studies; an inner seeking, a method is needed. No scripture is capable of giving you truth. What the scripture cannot give can be attained through inner seeking.

You should not take this to mean that I am saying all the scriptures are wrong. You shouldn't think that the scriptures do not contain the truth. What I am saying is that the truth cannot be attained through the scriptures. What I am saying is that you cannot have the truth by reading the scriptures. There are books about light, but they are useless for a blind man. I am not saying that what is written about light in those books is wrong, but his eyes cannot be opened through them. To open his eyes, a different treatment is required. If you keep this in mind, you will be able to understand what I am saying.

You cannot attain truth by reading anything. If truth could have been attained by reading, we would have opened schools for truth. That would not have been difficult; there you could have attained truth. People could have read the books and found truth.

Science can be achieved through study; religiousness cannot be achieved through study. Science books are helpful, and religious books are a hindrance. Science cannot be achieved without study. You can achieve everything about matter though study. There can be books about it. What relates to consciousness cannot be achieved through study. You can only experience it.

Along with this question, the same person has also asked:

> **Osho,**
> ***Man is not wise by birth; he has to study. What does he have to study to make his life successful?***

If you have understood what I have been saying just now, I would like to add that life succeeds not by studying the scriptures, but by studying life. Is there anything greater than the study of life? Haven't all the scriptures come from the study of life? When all thoughts are born from the study of life, would it not be better for us to study that life, rather than to gather secondhand information? If someone tells me something about love, will I come to know love? Don't I need to know love by myself, and experience it directly? Can I have the experience of love from someone else's love experience? While life is available, would it not be better to love in order to experience love?

When life has been given to us, we should study life itself – but we do not study life, we start studying the scriptures. They are completely dead. Life is in front of us, and we are studying scriptures.

There is an incident in the life of Rabindranath Tagore…

He was studying aesthetics. He was searching for what beauty is. He searched a lot and read many books, but he could not find a clear concept of what beauty is.

Once he spent a night in a houseboat. It was a full-moon night. He was sitting inside a room. He was sitting inside a small room and studying, reading about aesthetics. Around two o'clock he became tired. He shut the book, blew out the lamp and lay down in his chair. As he lay there, his eyes wandered toward the window. He stood up at once, went to the window and exclaimed, "Oh, what a fool I have been. Beauty was right in front of me and I was looking for it in books."

Beauty is always present, but there are madmen who look for it in books. Love is always present, but there are mad people who start to study even love from books. Existence is always present, but there are madmen who go to books to find it. What is this life that is all around us? Are God and truth and existence not present at each and every moment of life? They are, but we are neither ready to see them, nor do we wish to see them, nor do we have the background inside to see them.

I tell you that you are passing through life, but you are not able to see life. You will ask, "What are you talking about? We are alive day and night; we are alive from morning till evening; we are alive from evening till morning; we are alive around the clock" – and I am telling you that you go through life without knowing it.

Certainly, I am telling you that you are going through life without knowing it. That is why all these questions arise – whether there is a God or not. If you were acquainted with life, you would have found the godliness within you. That is why you ask whether there is a soul or not. That is why you ask if rebirth exists or not.

For the one who knows life, death disappears. Death cannot exist. But you do not know life. Is it not true that all of you, is it not true that all of us are afraid of death? If we knew life, would we be worried about death? Can life ever have a death? Can we call something that can die, life? Life is something that does not die. That which is life does not have an ending – but we are not acquainted with life.

Why are we not acquainted with life? We are not acquainted with life because life is always in the present, and we are either in the past or in the future. Life is always in the present. The three divisions of time are the past, which is gone; the future, which has not come yet; and the small moment of now, which is present. We are never in the living present. It is a very small moment. Before we can become aware, it has gone into the past. Our mind is in the past. Either we think about the past, or we think about the future. That is why we are deprived of the present, deprived of that which is, that which is in this very moment.

Once I took a friend of mine on a boat trip on the river and to the mountains. He had just come back after visiting foreign countries. He was a great poet who had traveled extensively. He had seen so many rivers and mountains; he had visited many beautiful places.

I took him for a sightseeing trip and he asked me, "What will be there? I have already seen many lakes, many beautiful mountains, and waterfalls."

I said, "Even so you should come with me. Why? – because I believe that everything has its own beauty. You cannot compare the beauty of one thing with the beauty of another, because in this world everything is unique; no two things are alike. Even a small pebble is unique in its own way. You can search the whole earth, and you will not find another piece of stone like that." I said, "Let us go. Let us go and see these small mountains and this small river."

I took him along with me. For two hours we traveled in a boat on that river in those mountains. All that time he was talking about the lakes in Switzerland. He was talking about the lakes in Kashmir. I kept on listening.

When we returned after two hours, he said, "It was a very beautiful place."

I put my hand over his mouth. I said, "Don't say anything more because I was there alone. You did not go. You were not there, only I was there."

He said, "What are you saying? I sat with you for two hours and we saw everything together."

I said, "You could be seen with me, but you were not with me. Your mind must have been in Switzerland, must have been in Kashmir, but it was not in those small mountains, that small river. You were not present. You did not see what was in front of you; your memory was running behind it. That which was present was hidden because of the movie of memory." I went on to say to him, "Now I have understood that what you say about the Swiss lakes must also be false, because I have understood your mind's habit; your mind must have been somewhere else when you were on those lakes."

That is the habit of all our minds. The mind is not where we are. The mind is where we are not. In that way, we are deprived of life. Either we keep thinking about the past, or we keep thinking about the future. In both states, we miss out on what is present. We are deprived of it. As I said, life is always in the present. Life is neither in the past, nor is life in the future.

Because of this mind that always roams in the past or the future, we remain unacquainted with the constant flow of life. Please study life. Do not let the mind dwell in the past. Do not let the mind wander unnecessarily in the future. Bring it back. Make it present to what is present. If you are sitting under the moon, remain with the moon for a while, and drop all worries of the past and the future from the mind. If you are sitting near a flower, just be with the flower for a while, and drop all thinking in the mind. Observe life and drop all thinking, and you will be surprised that what you were searching for in the scriptures has been constantly present and within reach. What you cannot attain from the scriptures is always within your reach.

We are absent. Remember, truth is always present, but we are absent. Existence is constantly present, but we do not face it. Either our eyes are shut, or they are wandering somewhere else.

I say, "Certainly study – but study life." The prerequisite for studying life is to drop thoughts and observe life directly.

Have you ever seen a face without thinking? Have you ever seen someone's eyes without thinking? Have you ever lifted up your eyes and seen the sun without thinking? Have you ever watched the ocean without thinking? A mountain, a hill, a flower, a tree, a road, people walking on the road, have you looked at anything without thinking?

If you do not look in that way, how will you become acquainted with life? You will be surrounded by your thoughts. Life is flowing by. Drop thinking and look, end thinking and look, let thoughts stop and look; what you see then is life. There is no greater study than that of life; no scripture is greater than that. If all the scriptures were erased, if all the scriptures were destroyed, even then the truth would not be destroyed. It is always present. If the scriptures were to increase – and they are increasing a lot… I have heard that about five thousand books are published in the world every week. Five thousand every week! Imagine what will happen after a while. There will be no space left for man, there will be so many books.

Even with all these books, what is happening? Where is man? Man continues to shrink every day. Books continue to increase, and man continues to shrink. Books will continue to increase, and man will become smaller. Slowly, slowly there will be mountains of books – and man's knowledge of life? Man's knowledge of life will become empty. Life is studied neither through the scriptures nor through words, it is studied through just being aware of life, through just being awake.

I am saying this in the way I understand it. I hope you understand what I am saying. If you have to study something, study life. Life is an open book of God. People say God wrote the Vedas. People say that God sent his only son Jesus Christ and wrote the Bible. All this is mad talk. God has written only one book, and that is the book of life. There is no other book written by God. Man's signature is on all other books. All other books were written by the hands of man. There is only one book of life that is written by God. If you have to call it the Vedas, do that; if you have to call it the Bible, do that. Study life, which is the book of God. Know it, recognize it, and do not let other books come in between. If other books come in between, you will be kept from studying life. Do not let any book come in between, and look at life directly. If you want to come in direct contact with godliness, why do you need to consult a book? Is it a school? Why do you need to burden yourself with books?

Someone has Ramayana in between him and existence; someone has the Bible; someone has the Vedas. All these books are very thick, and they will not let you face God. Throw them away. When godliness can be received directly, why do you put a book in the middle? Why do you put a book in between? There is no need to bring anything in between – neither a book, nor a master, nor a tirthankara, nor an avatar, nor a son of God. There is no need to bring anyone in between. The one who does so will remain deprived of life.

I am reminded of a small story…

Once there was a Sufi mystic. One night he had a dream that he suddenly reached heaven. He arrived in the land of God. There were lots of festivities going on. The whole road was crowded with people, filled with big lights and flags, and the whole place was well-lit and decorated; some kind of festival was going on. He stopped at the side of the road and asked someone what was happening. Millions of people were crowded there, and he asked someone what was happening. The man replied, "God is being brought out in a procession; it is his birthday today."

The mystic said, "How lucky I am that I came today and had the opportunity to see this occasion."

Then another very big crowd, a very big procession, came on the road. Lord Buddha was sitting on a horse and millions of people were following him.

The mystic asked someone, "Has the procession of God come?"

The man replied, "No, this is only the procession of Buddha; his followers are walking behind him."

Then it was followed by the procession of Rama; then by Mahavira's; then by Christ's; then by Krishna's; then by Mohammed's – and each one of them was followed by millions of people.

The mystic asked, "Where is the procession of God?"

The people replied, "These are only the processions of his incarnations, of his beloveds."

The mystic thought, "When his incarnations have such big processions, what will God's procession be like?"

Finally, after everyone else's procession had passed, he saw a very dead-looking horse coming, on which a very old man was seated.

The mystic asked, "Why hasn't the procession of God come yet?"

The people said, "What you are seeing now is the procession of God."

No one was with him. He was left all alone because some people had gone with Rama, some with Krishna, some with Mahavira, some with Buddha, some with Christ, some with Mohammed – and no one was with him, he was left alone. No one was accompanying his procession. It was supposed to be his birthday, and no one was joining his procession.

That is what has happened. Books and masters and incarnations and the son of God have come in between, in spite of the fact that any contact with God has to be direct and immediate.

With love you have to have a direct contact. No one can come in the middle with love. If I am in love with someone and another person is in the middle, how can love happen? If I pray and another person is in the middle, how can prayer happen? I am in love with someone and there is an agent in the middle; how can love happen? Love has to be direct. There can be no one in the middle. Prayer is also love. It is infinite love. It is also done directly. There can be no one in the middle – neither a book, nor words, nor a master.

Please remove whoever is in the middle. Please put them aside. If you want to reach godliness and truth, remove everyone from the middle. You are enough, alone. You alone are enough. Just study life and know life. Only what you receive from life is truth. Only what you receive from life is alive. Only what is received from life liberates.

Someone has asked:

> **Osho,**
> ***Should we derive our practice of inner discipline from the concept of samadhi, in Hatha yoga, Raja yoga, or some other path?***

Does samadhi have many types? Is the samadhi of Hatha yoga different from the samadhi of Raja yoga?

We have made divisions in everything and have put labels on everything. We have made gradations in everything. We have the customs of the marketplace in our minds. There, everything has a label on it. Everything has a separate box; everything has a separate shelf. We apply the same practice to religion. Our attitude is the same for everything; we think that everything consists of different divisions.

There was a Baul mystic in Bengal who was a devotee of Vishnu. The Bauls talk of love; they say that love is everything. Love is God. Once, a great pundit came to see him and asked, "Do you know how many kinds of love there are?"

The Baul said, "Love, and of different kinds? I have never heard of such a thing. I know of love, I do not know anything about any kinds of love."

The pundit said, "That means you do not know anything at all. Your life has been wasted. In our scriptures it is written that there are five kinds of love. You do not even know how many kinds of love there are, so how can you know what love is?"

The Baul mystic replied, "If it is written like that in the scriptures, it must be right. Perhaps I am wrong. I only know of love and have no idea about any different kinds. Since you are speaking anyway, I am willing to listen. Please read your holy book to me."

The pundit opened his scripture and told him how many types of love there were. He explained all the types of love to him. After he had explained the whole thing, he asked the mystic, "Have you understood what I told you? Has it had any effect on you?"

The Baul started to laugh, and he asked, "Has it had any effect on me? When you were reading your scripture, it appeared to me as if a goldsmith had brought his touchstone to a garden to test the flowers and see which flower was real and which flower was fake. That is how I felt." The Baul said, "You are mad! Can love ever have different types? Can there be love when there are types?"

Love is only one. Enlightenment is also only one. There cannot be twenty-five types of enlightenment. There are many types of diseases, you must remember, but there is only one type of health. There are many kinds of disturbances, there is only one kind of peace. There are many types of problems, but only one type of enlightenment.

Those who have a bookish mind make divisions; they analyze, that it is of this or that type – the Raja yoga type, or the Hatha yoga type, or the Bhakti yoga type, and so on. There are no types of Yoga or anything of the sort. There is only one Yoga. All those divisions were created by pundits; they are not the understanding of a disciple. A pundit takes great delight in analyzing things. If you were to read the scriptures, you would find very subtle divisions. They have been analyzed and divided in detail, but it is all just talk. There are crazy people who are very impressed by divisions and analyses; they think that it is something very special.

In life there are no divisions; life is one. Enlightenment is also one. What is the meaning of samadhi? Samadhi means that the mind is so peaceful that there is no problem left, there is no disturbance left. The mind is totally empty, so there is no activity left, there is no distortion left, there is no discontentment left. When the mind attains such a state of equanimity that there is absolutely no movement and no turmoil, what is known in that supreme state of peace is truth. Samadhi is the door to truth.

Enlightenment does not have any types, and neither does Yoga have any types. Those divisions, those categories of the scriptures are ours. We cling to them and we think there must be divisions.

There are no categories. I will say more about that tomorrow – when I talk then about emptiness of mind, I will say more about samadhi too. And I'll try to explain it further, so that you can grasp my point.

In life all these things are one. If there appear to be many types of enlightenment or Yoga, there is a mistake in our way of looking. We are certainly making a mistake. From those many names, many sects are made, and many faiths. They have their followers and their opponents also, and then turmoil is created in the world. Truth is pushed off to one corner, and people are busy discussing their opinions of truth.

Once a man went to a Zen master and told him that he wanted to know the truth. The master asked, "Do you want to know truth, or do you want to know about truth?" If you want to know about truth, you should go somewhere else. You will find many people who will tell you about truth. If you want to know truth, you should stay here, but you should not ask me again about truth."

The man was shocked. He said, "I agree. I have come here to know truth. I will stay."

The master told him, "This commune has five hundred monks and rice is cooked for them every day. Go and live in the hut behind the kitchen. Your job will be to clean the rice every day. There is no need for you to do anything else. There is no need for you to talk too much to anyone, to gossip with anyone. We will not give you monks' robes. You have only to clean the rice, and you should remember only one thing – when you are cleaning the rice, you should be doing only that and nothing else. Do only that. When you get tired, go to sleep, and when you wake up, do your job once again. That is all. You should not come to me again. If there is a need, I will come to you."

Three years went by. The man went on cleaning the rice. No one in the commune was even aware of him and his job. The other inhabitants of the commune thought about what enlightenment was, what truth was. They debated; the scriptures were read. The man who only cleaned rice stayed in the background. He had nothing to do with the scriptures. He did not talk to anyone. All five hundred inhabitants of the commune thought he was a simpleton, mad. "He just goes on cleaning his rice. Who is he, a servant?"

Slowly, slowly everyone forgot about him. Who would remember such a man? People only remember someone who makes a noise and creates a disturbance. The poor fellow kept cleaning the rice peacefully in the background. Who was going to remember him? Everyone forgot about him. They did not even know that he existed. He was just one of the objects in the commune.

Almost ten years went by. He never talked with anyone and never engaged in any of the commune debates. He just went on cleaning the rice and then went to sleep. In the beginning, for some time, old thoughts would go on moving in his mind. He simply went on cleaning the rice, so that new thoughts could not be born. He never gathered any new thoughts. For how long could the old thoughts keep on circulating? He cleaned his rice; his attention was always on the rice. When the bamboo stick was raised, his mind would rise with it and when the bamboo stick fell on the rice, his mind would fall with it. When he picked up the rice, his mind would pick up the rice; when he put down the rice, his mind would put it down. When he ate his food, his mind would eat the food; when he went to sleep, his mind would fall asleep.

Twelve years went by in this way. In those twelve years, who knows how many pundits the commune must have produced, how much knowledge they must have gathered – and that poor man remained as ignorant as before.

After twelve years, the master was getting old. One day, he announced in the commune that he would be leaving his body in a couple of days, and he wanted someone to be his successor.

He said, "The disciple who is worthy to take my place will be my successor. As a test, I would like all of you to write four lines on truth on a piece of paper and give it to me. If I feel that someone has the experience of the truth and has given the correct answer, I will make him my successor. He will take my place. Remember one thing: you cannot deceive me. If anyone tries to answer from the scriptures… I will recognize at once which answer has been copied from the scriptures, and which answer has come from the person himself. So do not try to deceive me."

Everyone in the commune knew that the master would know and could not be deceived. After a lot of hesitation, one disciple had the courage to write something down, because he was considered to be the most learned of the disciples. Even he did not have the courage to take his answer directly to the master. In the middle of the night when no one was looking, he got up like a thief and wrote his answer on the wall of the commune. He wrote four lines.

After writing the four lines he immediately ran away, and he did not sign his name underneath because he thought that they might possibly be from the scriptures after all. He himself was in doubt; he knew he did not have any experience of the truth inside. He wrote that the mind is like a mirror on which the dust of thoughts and distortions gathers. If the dust is removed, one will come to perceive the truth.

What he had written was correct. However, when the master saw it in the morning he shouted, "Who is the madman who spoiled the wall?"

Even we would say that it was the right answer, but the master shouted, "Who is the madman who spoiled the wall? Catch that man and bring him to me!"

The disciple had not put his name on it. He was hiding so that no one would know it was from him because the master had said, "It is all nonsense from the scriptures. The man learned it from some scripture or other."

The news spread through the whole commune. It happened that two disciples were discussing the affair when they went past the man who cleaned the rice. They were saying, "What a unique statement! He wrote that the mind is like a mirror on which the dust of thoughts and distortions gathers, and if you remove the dust you will realize the truth. He wrote such a unique statement, and the master still says it is all nonsense. What will happen now? Will the master's place remain vacant?"

The man who was cleaning the rice laughed. No one had ever seen him laugh before.

They asked him, "Why are you laughing?"

He replied, "Just like that, it is nothing."

"Even so, there must be some reason for laughing."

He replied, "The master is right. That man has ruined the wall."

No one had ever heard him speak before. They asked him, "You fool; do you know what the right answer is?"

He replied, "I have forgotten how to write. I will tell it to you, and you write it down," and he told it. He said, "The mind has no mirror at all; on what would the dust gather? The man who knows that truth, knows the truth." "Write that down."

The master came running to him and fell at his feet. He said, "I was waiting for this day. You were my only hope."

This is a man who attained samadhi. Those who are interested in the scriptures only read scriptures. That man attained enlightenment.

There is only one samadhi, for which slowly, slowly thoughts should somehow cease. The mind should slowly, slowly disappear. What remains after the mind has disappeared is truth. The moment you stumble upon the truth, you immediately attain enlightenment. It does not matter where you began and how you attained it. The essence of samadhi is only this, that the mind and thoughts should be empty. What remains is the soul, is truth, is enlightenment. You can give it any other name you want. Names do not make any difference.

Osho,
Do enlightenment, truth-realization and God-realization all have the same meaning?

Absolutely the same meaning. If you ask the pundits, they will say that they have totally different meanings. You say "God." A Jaina will say there is no God at all.

You say "soul." The Buddhists will ask, "What soul? – there is no such thing as a soul."

You say "truth." Someone will say, "Truth? – the truth cannot be put into words."

Soul, truth, and God all appear to be different. "That which is" does not have a name. A name is only a makeshift arrangement. You can give it any name.

Do you think the name you have is your name? Do you think the name a thing has is its own name? A name has been given to it. It has been put on it. It is only a makeshift arrangement. If someone calls you Rama, if your parents call you by that name, you become Rama. Do you think that then your name is Rama? Were you born with a name? Will you die with a name? It is only a label that has been put on you from the outside. It is a poor quality label; it does not have any sticking power at all. If you pull a little, it will come off. There is no problem; if you want, you can go to the court, deposit a few rupees, and change your name.

A name does not have any meaning. No one has a name. Everyone is nameless. A name is a man-made invention.

Mankind has invented some things, and names are one of them. It is the most dangerous invention, but very necessary, so you have to use it. No one has a name; how can the totality, the existence of the whole world have a name?

We name our children. There is something wrong with our minds; they have a habit of naming everything. These days we even give names to our houses. The same old habit is functioning. We name our children, name houses, name roads, name crossings, and name our gods too. Our minds have the habit of naming because without a name, how will we recognize someone? So we give him some name or other. Then we start fighting over names, because someone else starts giving something a different name, and a third person calls it still something else.

It is just as if a child has two or three fathers who cannot decide who his real father is, and each one gives him a different name. Then they all start to fight about which name is his. That is the condition God is in also. He is your father; he has many sons and they have each given him a name, and each one claims that his name is the real one.

There is no name at all. "That which is" has no name. You can call it truth, you can call it the soul, or God. The names are different only because we have given different names. So it is better if we say truth, or more correct if we say "that which is." If you feel love for it, you can call it God, you can call it the soul, but remember that it has no name. If there were no human beings in this world, nothing would have a name. Names are an invention of man.

Names have created a lot of problems. They have created a lot of difficulties; they have raised many difficulties. So many people have died for the sake of a name. So much killing has been done for the sake of a name. People start fighting because someone calls God, Allah, and someone else calls God, Rama.

Do you know how much madness has been caused because of names? If you were to think about this madness, you would be amazed that a world that fights over names is calling itself religious – a crazy world that fights over names!

Once, a friend of mine was my guest. He was a monk. In the morning, he said to me that he wanted to go to a temple. I asked him, "Why do you want to go?"

He said, "I want to sit in solitude and have some peace. I want to remember God for a while."

I told him that the temple there was located in the market, in a very crowded locality where there would be a lot of noise. However, the church was right next door, so it would be better if he went to the church. There would be plenty of peace and solitude there. No one was inside, and there would be no problem.

He replied, "What, a church? What are you saying?"

I said, "Except for the name, what is the difference? If you buy a sign tomorrow, you can remove the sign saying *Church* and call it *Temple*, and it will become a temple. After all, it is only a building. Does the name make any difference?"

Recently one of my friends bought a church in Kolkata and converted it into a temple, so it became a temple. Until the day before, Christians were going there, now no Christian goes there. Now Jainas are going there – and until the day before, no Jaina would even dream of going there. Such is the madness – a name! The building is still the same, the walls are the same, the floor is the same. Everything is the same, but now it is a temple; then it was a church. Then it was the abiding place of a certain God, now it has become the abiding place of a different God – as if there were many gods.

Our clinging to names goes very deep. It is childish, immature, like a child who keeps clinging to things. For the sake of a name we will take out our swords; we are willing to kill people and destroy countries, to set fire to everything, to destroy everything.

In this world, no one has done as much brutality and as much stupidity as we have done in the name of religion; and all of it is done just for the sake of names. Even after all that, our eyes do not open. Even after all that, we go on shouting about names and keep clinging to them. We have committed unaccountable destruction for the sake of names.

I want to make it very clear to you that a name is a very illusory thing. A name has no meaning. See truth, do not see the name. Otherwise you will get stuck on the name, and you will not be able to see truth. Drop the name and see what the meaning is. That is why I use all names simultaneously here. I use expressions such as "a vision of God," self-realization, or "coming upon the truth," so that people who use different names can understand that I am talking about the same thing. If I say "a vision of God," some people will take it to mean that I belong to the Hindu religion, and so on. If I say self-realization, some people will be uncertain about which religion I belong to, since I do not talk about a God.

I am using them all simultaneously on purpose, so that you get the point. "That which is" has no name. You have only to think about it; you have only to experience it; you have only to enter it, only to realize it. Drop all names and become aware of the nameless. Be aware of whatever has no name. Awaken to whatever has no form. Bring your awareness to whatever is not confined to any place, to any boundaries; to whatever is not limited, is not in any name, in any form. Only that is; whether you call it God, or the soul, or truth, does not really matter.

Osho,
Why does the mind commit sin, and who is the father of sin?

It will be a little difficult for me to explain this to you. In fact, only you are the father of sin. How could anyone else be the father? Although you feel like saying it is someone else. You want me to say that someone else is the father of sin. It is you – and when I say it is you, I mean that it is only you. I am not talking about your neighbor. I am talking directly to you, not to the person who sits next to you.

Why do we commit sin? The truth is that no one in the world commits sin. Sin happens. Neither sin can be done, nor virtue can be done. Virtue happens and sin also happens.

You have to understand this. Generally, we say that such and such a man is a sinner, and such and such a man does good deeds. That means we are under the impression that it is all in the hands of man; if someone wants, he can do good deeds and if he wants, he can commit a sin. When you commit a sin, have you ever thought that it was in your hands, that if you wanted to, you could have avoided committing it? If it was in your hands, why didn't you stop? When you became angry, did you know at the time that it was in your hands not to become angry? When a man kills someone, do you think it was in his power not to kill the man? Do you think that even though it was in his hands, he still went ahead and killed the man?

That is not my view. If a man is unconscious, he is bound to commit sin. Sin is a natural result of unconsciousness. No one commits sin; sin happens in unconsciousness. That is why there is no condemnation in my mind for a sinner.

When someone says that a person has committed a sin, it is actually that he wants to enjoy condemning someone. All the monks and honorable people of the world derive joy from condemning others as sinners. The more strongly they prove them to be sinners, the more they prove themselves to be virtuous. That is why condemnation has such appeal. Condemn someone else, say he commits sins and is a sinner. It is to hide their own sins that those who are deeply drowned in sin keep on shouting at others, saying that such and such a thing is a sin, that certain people sin, and that everyone should protect themselves against sinning.

When someone starts to shout that people should not sin, you take it to mean that he at least must not be a sinner. If a man commits a theft, and he himself starts shouting that a theft was committed, crying out, "Catch the thief," you will for sure not catch him. He is shouting about catching the thief, so he must not have committed the theft. He himself is shouting that a theft has been committed and that the thief has to be caught, so who will catch him? People will leave him be. The cunning keep shouting to others that so and so is a sinner. They themselves are the sinners, and all those actions are sins.

I say unto you that no man commits sins. Sin happens. When I say it happens, what I mean is that there is a state of mind that is unconscious. There is a state of mind in which it is not conscious. We are not conscious of what we are doing at all. Some actions just happen through us. Just try to remember: whenever you have been angry, did you do it? Did you think it over? Did you decide you would be angry? Did you will yourself to be angry at that moment? You did not do anything. You suddenly found yourself angry.

Once a mystic was passing through a village. He was passing through a market in which he had a few enemies. They got hold of him and started to abuse him terribly. They were very angry with him, and insulted him badly. After they had finished abusing him and insulting him, the mystic said to them, "Friends, I will be coming here again tomorrow to give you a reply."

His enemies were very surprised when they heard this. They had abused him terribly, insulted him, and uttered ugly words about him, and the man was telling them, "Friends, I will be coming here again tomorrow to give you a reply." He was saying, "Friends, I will be back tomorrow to give you a reply."

They asked him, "Are you mad? We are abusing you, we are insulting you; can anyone give a reply to abuses and insults the next day? Whatever you have to give, give it now."

The mystic said, "I never do anything in unconsciousness. I always use my intelligence; I ponder over things. I will think about it, and if I think it is necessary to become angry, I will express my anger. If I do not think it is necessary, I will not do it. It is possible that what you are saying might be right. The things you're saying about me might be true. In that case I will not come. Then I will say, 'It is correct; what they have said is correct.' In that case I will take it as a description of my character and not as condemnation. You have spoken the truth. If I think that it is necessary to be angry, then I will be angry."

They said, "You are a very strange man. Has anyone ever become angry after thinking about it? Anger only takes place without thinking, in the absence of mindfulness. No anger is ever experienced after thinking about it."

No sin can ever be committed after giving it thought. No sin can be committed consciously, when one is conscious. That is why I never say that sin is done; I say sin happens. You will say, "That means nothing is in our hands. If sin happens, what should we do? If anger happens, what can we do?" What should I tell you?

A killer will say, "What can I do about it? Killing just happens." It is true. There is no question of his doing it. On this level you do not have to do anything. When sin happens, it is an indication that the soul is asleep. At the level of sin, no change can take place; neither do you have to do anything, nor can it be done. It is only an indication of the fact that the soul is fast asleep inside. Your sin is on the outside; that indicates that the soul is asleep inside. It is a question of awakening the soul. It is not a question of changing the sin; it is a question of awakening the soul. What I am talking about here is how the soul can be awakened. When the soul has been awakened, you will find that sin disappears, and in its place virtue comes into being.

Virtue also happens, that too cannot be done. People generally say that when people stoned Mahavira, he forgave them. What they say is completely false. Can Mahavira forgive? Even if forgiveness happens, it is not done. Mahavira is in a state of awareness. Someone throws a stone, someone insults, within him only forgiveness happens. Where is the doing in this? With you, anger happens; with Mahavira, forgiveness happens. Forgiveness flows out of him, he is not doing it.

If you throw a stone at a tree full of flowers, the flowers fall down; if you throw a stone at a thorn tree, the thorns fall down. What is there is released, what is there falls down. Mahavira has only love inside him and nothing else. If you shout insults at him, what will he do? He will share only love. He can give only that which he has. Only that which can flow outward, flows.

In life, things emanate, they happen. They are not done. The people who say Mahavira forgave them are saying something completely false. Those who say Mahavira practiced nonviolence are saying something completely false. Those who say Buddha was compassionate are saying something false. They did not do anything; those things happened. They are in the state of consciousness where only compassion can flow.

The crowd crucified Christ. When he was on the cross, they asked him if he had a last wish. Christ said, "Father, forgive them, because they know not what they are doing." You will say that Christ was a very forgiving man. No, that was the only thing Christ could do. In the state of consciousness Christ was in, only this could have come out of him; nothing else could have happened.

Do you understand what I am saying? It is not the action that has value; it is your being, your inner state that has value. If you start clinging to actions, you keep going round and round. You think, "I should change my actions. What I am doing is a sin; I should change it, and I should do the right thing."

You cannot do anything. Someone whose consciousness is fast asleep inside can never do a virtuous act. As I said this afternoon, you might think that a man whose consciousness is fast asleep has done a great virtuous act when the crowd says he built a temple. That statement is completely false. Because the man's consciousness is fast asleep he did not build a real temple; rather he just built a memorial for his father, or he just built a memorial for his own name. He did not build a temple. What does he have to do with a temple? Because his inner consciousness is in a sleeping state, whatever he builds does not matter; in that state, sins are bound to happen.

According to me, whatever an unaware man does is sin. My definition of sin is anything done by an unconscious man. Whatever happens through a conscious man is virtuous. Even when an unconscious man tries to imitate virtue, then too it is sinful. In the same way, if an act of a man who is awake appears sinful to you, you should not be in a hurry to judge him; even that will be a virtue – it is a virtue. Sin cannot happen through him. There is no question of his committing a sin.

Perhaps you will understand my view. Not at the level of sin and virtue, but at the level of consciousness – a sleeping consciousness and an awakened consciousness, an awakened soul and a sleeping soul, an unconscious soul and a conscious soul – the whole matter is at that level. In both situations you are responsible, not for the act but for the state of your consciousness. Understand my difference. You have to bring change at a deeper level. At the surface, no change happens. There is no change at the level of doing; change happens at the very root of being, at the level of the soul.

That is why when someone says that a certain act is sin and another act is virtuous, I am surprised. Acts are neither good nor bad. The same act may be a sin and also a virtue. That can only be so when there is a difference in consciousness, when the consciousness is altogether different, when an awakened consciousness does the same thing as a sleeping consciousness does. The act is the same, but because of the difference in the level of consciousness, one is sin and one is virtue.

Acts are never sinful or virtuous; it is the state of mind. The real thing to be considered is the state of mind. That has to be practiced. It is only there that a revolution, a transformation, a change has to take place.

At our level, we only think a particular act is sin, and another act is virtue. A sinner starts thinking, "Let me do a virtuous act, a charitable deed, so I can become a virtuous man." He was sinning day and night, and then one day he builds a temple. Then he thinks, "I have done a virtuous deed." He sins day and night, and then he takes a bath in the holy Ganges. He thinks, "I have done a holy deed."

Once, a man asked Ramakrishna, "If I take a bath in the holy Ganges, will all my sins be washed away?"

Ramakrishna was a very simple and straightforward man. He thought, "What can I say? If I say they will not be washed away, I will be condemning the Ganges. Why should I condemn the Ganges for nothing? If I say they will be washed away, this dishonest man will think that he is going to take a bath in the Ganges and all his sins will be washed away – as if he has done a virtuous deed." Ramakrishna was a very simple man. He asked himself, "What should I do? This is putting me into difficulty."

He said to the man, "Brother, sins definitely get washed away in the Ganges because the Ganges is really a holy river. Sins get washed away in it, but the sins then jump into the trees that are standing on the shore and they sit there. When you come out of the Ganges, they jump on you again. After all, you will have to come out at some time. You will have to come out of the river; how long can you stay there? As long as you are in the river, you are safe. The moment you come out, they jump back onto you. Think about what will happen when you come out of the river."

There is no way you can do a virtuous act by taking a bath in the Ganges; or constructing a temple; or giving something to charity; or doing some social service; or building a hospital; or starting a school, or doing this or that. All that is not virtue because your very state of mind is that of a sinner. All the actions that come out of it are sinful. Pretending on the outside does not make any difference.

It can also happen that a man whose state of mind has been transformed may do something that seems wrong to you.

Gandhi gave poison to a calf. The whole country, which always thinks about nonviolence, was shocked and said he had committed a sin. Certainly, if you think about it, poisoning a calf is a sin. Is there any doubt about it? Why did Gandhi kill it? After all, Gandhi had as much intelligence as you do. He could also have known it was a sin. He had at least as much intelligence as you. Gandhi had at least as much intelligence as the people who said he had sinned. What was the matter?

Gandhi's act was not a sin, although it definitely appeared to be. It was out of Gandhi's love. People told Gandhi that if he gave the calf poison, there would be opposition in the whole country. He would be committing a sin by killing it, so he could also go to hell. Gandhi said that he did not care about going to hell; his love told him that the calf was in such great pain and he could not save it, so he took the responsibility upon himself to kill it.

"It is in such great pain; I cannot bear to see its pain, so I am taking the responsibility to kill it. It is certainly a sin, and I am willing to go to hell. At least the calf is released from its pain."

Your nonviolence will not be able to understand the level of Gandhi's love. Your nonviolence will say, "What are you talking about?"

Krishna said to Arjuna that he should kill and not be afraid. "Neither does anyone die, nor can anyone kill. No one dies. Even when you pierce someone with a sword, no sword can pierce him."

What Krishna is saying is absolutely right. However, if you think about it, you will ask what he is talking about. If you kill someone, will he not die? If you kill, will there not be a sin? What Krishna is saying is that no one can die. Your idea that you are killing someone is madness, is ignorance; it is foolishness. That does not mean you should go and kill someone. But on that level of consciousness everything is different. Even if Krishna kills someone, it will not be a sin.

However, if your help would make even ten sick people survive, it would be a sin if, after giving them a new lease on life, you immediately run to the newspaper office and tell them to print your name. "I have cured ten people of their illness." The question is not what you have done. The question is what you are.

The question is not what you have done. The question is what you are. Ponder over that: What are you? If your consciousness is asleep, all actions are sin. If your consciousness is awake, no action is a sin. My definition is this: an act that comes from a person who is awake is virtuous, and an act that comes from a person who is asleep is a sin.

There are a few small questions:

> ***Osho,***
> ***I know there is a conflict inside me. I want to erase it, but I do not have the patience to do so. What to do?***

The first thing is, suppose a man has fallen into a fire and we tell him to get out of the fire, otherwise he will be burned. If he says, "I know I am in a fire, but my mind does not feel like coming out," what will we tell him? He says, "I know I am in a fire, but my mind does not feel like coming out."

If this building catches fire, will you come and tell me, "I know the building is on fire, but my mind does not feel like getting out?" No, you will not stop running in order to ask me. No one will stop to ask anyone. No one will stay in the building; you will all be seen outside immediately.

You say you feel a conflict, but I tell you that you don't feel it yet. Otherwise there would be no room left to ask the question; you would jump out of it. You do not feel a conflict. Yes, when someone talks about having an inner conflict, you start thinking you must also have a conflict inside. People preach to you, books tell you, philosophers say it, so you feel there is a conflict. Do you feel it? If you feel it, who is giving birth to the conflict? If you feel it, who is creating it every day? If you feel it, who stops you from jumping out of it?

You say you don't have patience, but you do have the longing. The basic thing is that you do not really know what the inner conflict is. Have you ever observed your interiority, or have you only read about it in books? Have you ever turned in and recognized what is there? Or have you just built an image of yourself, and that is what you think understanding yourself is?

Inside every man there are at least three personalities. One is what he really is, about which he does not know anything. The second is what he thinks he is. The third is what he wants to project to people that he is. Every individual is divided into three levels. The first is the one he is really on, but is unaware of. The second is the one he considers himself on. The third is the one he wants others to believe he is on. In this way every individual is divided over three levels.

The real man is who you actually are. You think that you are very humble, and you are filled with ego inside. If you think you are very religious, inside you will be full of irreligiousness. If you think you are a man who does a lot of social service, from the inside you will always want everyone to serve you. Are you really the person you understand yourself to be? If you remain stuck at who you think you are, you will never come to know your real inner being.

Before he can come to know himself, a man has to become naked; he has to drop all his clothes. We not only wear clothes on the outside, we also wear clothes on the inside, in the mind. We are not only afraid to be naked on the outside, we are also very afraid to be naked on the inside. We are very afraid to see ourselves naked, to see what we really are. We should not see what we are, otherwise we will be afraid of ourselves. So we put on many faces and decorate ourselves in many ways; we make many arrangements to avoid seeing our real inner self.

Before anyone can wish to know his inner self, he needs to take off all these clothes. You need to remove the masks you are wearing and the faces you have put on. Then you can see yourself and you can recognize yourself. Then it does not take time to get out of the inner conflict, the restlessness, the anxiety, and the clash that you feel inside. Then coming out of the conflict is not a problem. It is very easy to come out of the conflict because you created it. No one else but you has put it there. Then you will see very clearly all the reasons for the conflict, and you will stop nourishing those reasons.

If I see that a thorn bush is growing in my house, that thorns are spreading through the whole house; and I continue to water its roots and fertilize it; and also put a fence around it so no animal eats it; and thorns are growing on the bush and poisoning the whole house; and the thorns continue to spread in the whole house and cause me great worry... If I then go out to tell someone that I am in very great difficulty because a thorn bush has grown in my house and it is spreading all over the house... If that person comes into my house and sees me watering the bush, giving it fertilizer, putting a fence around it so that no animal eats it and no harm is done to it, what do you think he will say to me? He will ask, "What is the matter with you? What are you doing? Are you out of your mind? Every day you continue to nourish the same thorns you are condemning."

We are not aware; we condemn the thorns, but we do not know we are also watering their roots. We don't know it because we have never taken hold of the thorns and traced them to their roots. If we were to take hold of the thorns and look inside them, we would be able to see their roots and we would stop watering them. Ultimately we would break the fence; we would stop watering the bush and fertilizing it, and the bush would dry up and die. There would be no roots and there would be no thorns. The thorns are pricking us, and we don't know anything of their roots.

Go inside your mind. Wherever you see a conflict, go into it, go inside, and reach where the conflict is.

On the day I arrived here, a young man came to visit me and said his mind was very tense. He asked me to please tell him some way to make his mind peaceful.

I asked, "Why do you want to make it peaceful?"

He said, "I am going to take an examination for the Indian Administrative Services. I want to come first in the examination. I want to be calm so I can achieve first place in the examination."

I said, "Look, if you give water to the roots and deny the thorns, it will be difficult. Where there is a feeling of competition, there is tension. When you want to be ahead of others, you yourself are causing the tension. You say you do not want to be tense, but you want to be ahead of others. That is very difficult; it is contradictory. Only someone who is willing to be last, who does not worry about getting ahead can be peaceful. Otherwise he has to choose tension. Why are you worried? When you want to come first, tension will be the result; it is bound to be. Accept that you will be tense, and go ahead and compete. If you want to compete and also want to be peaceful so that you can compete well, there is a problem."

Christ said, "Blessed are those who have the courage to be last" – the courage to be last – "They are blessed, for in the eyes of God, they will be first." The point is that those who have the courage to come last are very few. Very few people have that much courage. There is nothing great in having the courage to come first. It is normal; everyone wants to come first. There is nothing of great value in the courage to come first. To become the president of a country does not need much courage, it is a very ordinary thing. Everyone wants to be something. Every ordinary man would like to be president. After all, some ordinary man does become president. There is no value in it. The value lies in having the courage to be last, because only a very rare man is able to do that. Christ said,

"Blessed are those who have the courage to be last. In the eyes of God they are standing first."

I told that young man, "On the one hand you are in a competition and you are nourishing that competition, and on the other hand you say you want to have peace. You don't know that the thorn of disturbance is rooted in competition."

I have said this as an example. Go inside your mind. Look into your mind; understand your mind. Wherever you find that there is a difficulty, behind it you will find that you are the one who is watering it. When you can see that it is you who is nourishing it, then it is in your hands. If you want to have thorns, give it more water; if you don't want to have thorns, stop giving it water. You don't have to accept someone else's decision; it is your own decision. If you know your inner world rightly, there will be no need to ask anyone else.

Because we don't know our inner self, we ask others. We want to keep the roots and remove the thorns. That creates all the conflict and tension. There is no real problem with anybody. There is only one difficulty: nobody knows his inner self totally. It works in two ways. You want to remove the thorns and you simultaneously give water to the roots. You want to cultivate good qualities, but you never try to find out where the roots of those good qualities lie; you want to paste on the good qualities from the outside. You want to remove bad habits, but you do not see their roots, which you continue to water.

The more trimming you do from the outside... You should know – even an ordinary gardener knows this – that anything you trim becomes thicker. Whatever you trim from the outside becomes denser, and its roots become thicker. You trim it from the outside, and give it water from underneath. That leads your life into discomfort, problems, and conflict.

Please try to understand. There is no one who can help you, there is no one who can give you a mantra or a good luck charm that you can tie around your wrist to be peaceful. Neither does starting to chant "Rama, Rama" help you to be peaceful; nor does going to a temple and lighting lamps, performing the rituals of worshipping your deity lead you to peace; nor does traveling somewhere; nor does giving a cow to charity make you peaceful. Do not ever fall into that type of madness. No one can become peaceful like that. In order to be peaceful, you have to dissolve all your inner contradictions. That is real spiritual discipline. Superficial changes such as renouncing clothes, or dying clothes in fanciful colors and so on, things like that should not be taken as spiritual practices. Neither does one become peaceful by doing all that, nor is purity of consciousness attained like that.

For the real problems of life to be solved, don't think of running away from them. Come to grips with the problems, recognize them, enter them, know them, and penetrate right down to the ends of their roots. That is science. That is how to transform life; that is how to take life upward. By entering a problem and recognizing and taking hold of its roots, transformation will start. Then the decision will be clear. If you want to keep the thorns, give them water; if you don't want to have the thorns, stop giving them water. It is as simple as that. It is certainly that simple.

There will have to be some kind of effort. You will have to make an effort to turn inward. You will have to show a little courage to go inside. People are not as afraid to travel on unknown roads as they are of entering themselves, and there is a reason for that fear. You have put on a false face. As you start going inside, your entire structure will come apart, and the person you see there will be terrifying.

Someone is sitting like a holy man, and thousands of people believe he is a holy man. How can he go inside? If he goes inside, he will encounter the Devil, so he starts to worry. How to go inside? If he goes inside, he will find a sinner sitting there – and on the outside he is a holy man. So he decides that he should forget about going inside. He should somehow stay outside, and let the time pass like that. He finds ways to remain outside.

That is the reason we all find ways to stay outside. We fear going inside because we are afraid when we go inside. If we really want to end the conflict inside, we must go inside that conflict.

I trust that some of what I have been saying must have become clear to you. If you have any other questions about this, I will take them up in the morning.

I have received many questions. Some of them have remained unanswered. Some questions must remain unanswered, because who am I to answer all your questions? There is no one who can answer all questions. Even when I answer your questions, you should not think your questions will be solved. I am only sharing my point of view. Perhaps you will be able to grasp my point of view.

A particular question and its answer are not all that valuable. A question is a question, and an answer is an answer. In themselves they are not very valuable, but the insight through which I am giving the answer is. Don't cling to the answer; rather I would like you to have a sense of the insight, the angle, and the position from which I see life. If you can have a glimpse of that insight, you have found the answer – not only to the questions I have answered, but also to the questions I have not answered.

If you cannot see my insight, then you would do better to prepare an answer yourself in my name. This is not a school exam where questions are given to children and they prepare and write down the answers. In fact, preparing answers and writing them down is not even real education. It is fake education – but let us leave that topic aside for now.

In life you cannot learn answers, you can only learn points of view. All the effort I am making here is not to give you a ready-made formula you can memorize. In that case I would be contradicting myself, because that is exactly what I am speaking against. You know a lot of ready-made formulas already. Drop them. Try to understand a different approach to seeing life. If you can grasp that quality of perception, it will not be my answer but your perception that will give you the answer. The answer that comes out of your inner perception is the only real answer. All other answers are meaningless.

I trust you have understood what I have said. You are listening to me with so much love. A few things I have spoken about may seem bitter to swallow. In fact, not a few, but most of them. Even then you listened to me with love; that shows your compassion for me. That you listened even to the bitter parts of what I have said with so much love shows your kindness toward me. In the old days, people would have thrown stones at me, or done something even worse. The world has become a little better, and the human being has become a little better; he listens with love. That is great kindness.

Existence is very compassionate to make the world a better place now. Otherwise it would have been difficult to say even this much; you would have caught me by the neck. When you are so kind to me, I feel very grateful to you. You listened even to my bitter statements with so much silence. By the grace of existence, please ponder over them, and think about them just a little. Never believe in them; think about them and try to understand them. The day you feel such an approach is right for you, that day a door will open inside you. That door will be yours. It will not be mine. At that moment you will see something that is yours. It will not be mine.

I am saying all this with the hope that perhaps someone, somewhere, might be ready, and something might open up in him. Some knot might loosen up a little; even that will be of great significance.

Please accept my thanks and my greetings to the divine within you.

4
Emptiness of Mind

Today we will discuss emptiness of mind. What we know as life is not life. What we believe to be life – we live it and then die – is not life. Very few fortunate people are able to experience life. For those who are able to experience life, there is no death. As long as there is death and the fear of death, as long as you feel you will come to an end, that you will be annihilated, know that you are not in touch with life, not in contact with life – and you have not experienced life.

I would like to start today's talk with a small story. I have told this story many times, to many people in different parts of the country, still I want to tell it again because I feel there is something in the story that everyone should know.

Jesus Christ was on a journey. He was sharing with others what he had attained. It is in the nature of bliss that if you attain it, you are bound to share it unconditionally. Suffering makes one shrink and bliss makes one expand. In suffering, one wants to be enclosed in himself; in bliss, he wants to reach out to everyone, he wants to expand to all. Thus we have called bliss, *brahman*. Suffering is the extreme of the ego; bliss is the extreme of the state of selflessness, of being *brahman*, that which is always expanding.

You may have noticed that when Buddha, Mahavira, and Christ were suffering, they ran away to the forest; and after they attained bliss, they returned to the marketplace. Bliss wants to be shared, suffering wants to withdraw. Suffering wants to be enclosed in itself and bliss wants to expand to others.

When Christ attained bliss, he embarked on a journey to share it with others. It was early in the morning and he was going to a village. He saw a fisherman on the shore catching fish; he had thrown his net in the lake and was waiting for the fish to come. The man did not know who was standing behind him. Christ approached him and, putting his hand on his shoulder, asked him, "Friend, look at me. How long will you keep on catching fish?"

Just like Christ, I would also like to put my hand on everyone's shoulder and ask them the same thing, "How long will you keep on catching fish?" What difference does it make whether you are catching bread or catching fish? It is all the same. Most people spend their lives just catching fish.

Christ asked him, "How long will you keep on catching fish?"

The man turned around; he had been looking into the lake behind him and now he looked into the eyes of the man standing in front of him, whose eyes were deeper than the lake. He thought, "I should throw away the net in the lake, and throw another net into those eyes." He threw away the net immediately and followed Christ. He said, "I will follow you. If there is something other than fish to catch, I am ready to catch it. I am throwing away this net here and now, and give up these fish right away."

Whoever wants to search for religiousness must have that much courage. When the time comes, he must throw away the net and the fish.

The man began to follow Christ. They had hardly reached the outskirts of the village when a man came running up to the fisherman and asked him, "Where are you going? Your father, who was sick, died last night. He just died. You must come home at once. We have been searching for you everywhere."

The young fisherman said to Christ, "Forgive me, I have to go back and attend the funeral of my father. I will come back in a few days."

Christ held his hand and said to him, "Follow me. Let the dead bury their dead. The dead people in the village will bury their dead. Come follow me." Christ said, "The dead, who are the majority in the village, will bury their dead. What is the need for you to go back?"

He said a very strange thing; and very meaningful also. Certainly those who are not in contact with life are dead. We know nothing about life. What we call life is only a gradual death. It is not actual life. The day we are born and the day we die and what is spread in between them is not life; it can only be called a gradual death. We are dying every day. What we call life is dying every day. It is a gradual death.

Death is not a sudden happening; it starts with the day of our birth. The day of our birth is also the day of our death. We start dying from that very day. The moment we are born, dying begins. Death keeps growing more and more, and one day it is complete. The day it is complete, we say that death has come. Death was coming every day; otherwise how could it have suddenly arrived? Death was coming every day, and one day it is complete.

Birth is the beginning of death, and death is the completion of death. Neither is birth the beginning of life, nor is death the end of life. Life was there before birth and will also be there after death. The one who lives only between that birth and death is not actually alive. Only someone who becomes connected with the life that is before birth and beyond death is alive. True religiousness is concerned with discovering truth, connecting one with that which is never born and never dies.

We have talked about two steps to move toward that life. In the first step, I spoke of being free from all scriptures, from all theologies, and from all thoughts. An intelligence that is burdened with the weight of the scriptures cannot attain its own individuality. An intelligence that is burdened with the thoughts of others is never able to awaken its own power of thinking. An intelligence that thinks others' understanding – whether Mahavira's or Krishna's or Rama's – is its own, has neither recognized nor actualized its own wealth of understanding.

That is why I told you to be free from all thoughts, no matter where they come from. Whether they come from great people or great scriptures or some other great pious books does not matter; those thoughts are outsiders to you. Anyone who tries to live while believing those thoughts to be his own will be deprived of the capacity to think – a capacity that is always present inside him and that wants to be manifested. The thoughts that come from outside don't allow it to be manifested.

Before someone's own thinking awakens, he must be empty of thoughts. Before someone can know his own wealth of understanding, he must be free of others' wealth of understanding. It is natural, it is only natural that if we take others' wealth of understanding to be our own, the search for our own wealth will stop. Many people get so completely lost in scriptures, theologies about truth, and doctrines that their own search stops; it comes to nothing.

Always remember, as I have mentioned, that if you want to search for truth you have to do it yourself. No one can give it to anyone else. Truth is not transferable. Truth is something which cannot be transferred from one hand to another hand. If it could have been transferred, everyone would have it by now. Truth cannot be given; truth has to be attained. Truth has to be attained by oneself. It is attained only by one's own effort. Those who believe in others' efforts waste their lives. They are not able to attain anything at all. That's why I told you to free yourself from others, so that your intelligence is free and your mind is free. How can someone whose mind is imprisoned know truth? I talked about this in detail in the first step.

In the second step, I talked about simplicity of mind. By simplicity, I don't mean that by wearing fewer clothes or eating less food you will become simple, or that by renouncing your house and belongings you will become simple. Simplicity is a very deep thing. Simplicity does not have much to do with all those trivia. Very complicated people, full of complexes, with very complicated, complex minds hard as stone, may also change their way of dressing and behave in a simple way. They may eat less, wear light clothes and renounce their homes. Even a complicated man can impose such a type of simplicity on himself. That simplicity does not have any value.

By simplicity, I mean that the mind should become free from all conflict, all fragmentation of the mind should disappear, and the mind should become integrated; it should be whole. You should not have many people inside; a single individual should be born within you. You should be an individual. You should have only one note left inside you. When there is love inside, there should not be any hatred. The mind of a man who has love and hatred side by side inside cannot be simple. The mind of a man who has both peace and tension inside cannot be simple. If only one of the two remains, the mind can be simple. If only disturbance is left, the mind will be simple; if only peace remains, the mind will also be simple.

Did you know that if someone is so tense that not even a glimmer of peace is left inside him, a revolution will happen?

With that much tension there is also a revolution. When reaching the peak of tension, in that climax also, everything suddenly disappears and the mind immediately becomes peaceful.

It is just like shooting an arrow; you pull the string backward. The arrow has to be shot forward, but you pull it back. You appear to be doing the opposite. Someone can say you have to shoot the arrow forward, but you pull it back. If you have to send it forward, send it forward; why pull it back? Why do the opposite? – but the archer keeps pulling his string back. Then a point comes when he cannot pull it back any more. The ultimate point of pulling back has been reached and the string is released, and the arrow that had moved backward starts to move in the opposite direction. In the same way, if the mind becomes completely tense, when it reaches the ultimate point of tension, the arrow is shot and it moves in the direction of peace.

Blessed are those who are totally tense because peace will be theirs. But we are always half-hearted; we are not totally tense. We are somewhat satisfied and somewhat peaceful. That kind of mind is mediocre, it is difficult; that kind of mind is complex. It has both. It has peace and tension also; love and hatred also, and everything else too. This duality does not let us move toward truth. Only if the mind becomes totally silent can truth be experienced in life.

Revolution happens at the extremes. No revolution happens in the middle. The mediocre person always stays far away from the truth. Revolution happens at the extremes. Extreme suffering throws a man out of suffering – but we never suffer to the extreme. We forget every suffering; we always find some way to explain away every suffering.

Someone's son died and he came to me and said, "I am suffering very much."

I said, "Suffer more. Suffer totally, and transformation will take place."

"No," he replied, and he asked, "Can you tell me whether the soul of my dead son is immortal or not?"

I said, "You are inventing tricks to make your suffering less. If someone can make you believe that rebirth exists – the boy is not dead, there is nothing to worry about, his soul is immortal, his new birth has taken place somewhere else – your mind will be at peace. Your suffering will be halted in the middle and no transformation will happen. You will explain away the suffering. You will find some way out."

Many people keep asking if reincarnation exists. They do not ask because they are interested in knowing about reincarnation. They ask because they see people dying every day, and they become afraid that they will also have to die one day. So they ask, "Is there such a thing as rebirth?" If you can make them believe in it, they will touch your feet and tell you that you are a very great soul, a very great saint. "You have put my mind at peace."

Whoever asks that has not made his mind peaceful. He has compromised. He could have gone through suffering by confronting death, and he has avoided that suffering. That suffering could have brought about a revolution. The doctrine of reincarnation will not bring about any transformation.

In our lives we always stop in the middle. We never allow anything to go to its extreme. I say to you, "If you have to be angry, be totally angry. Observe, and in one bout of total anger there will be a revolution. At the point of total anger, you will find that anger has disappeared." There are extreme points of evaporation. It is just like when someone heats water: at a hundred degrees it will definitely become steam. If you stop at fifty degrees, neither will the water remain water, nor will it be able to become steam. It will remain only lukewarm.

I spoke of how simplicity in life is born when the whole life force is centered at any one point, and a state of non-duality comes into being. I talked about how to create an integrated life. In the second step, I explained to you how that can be brought about.

Today I would like to talk to you about the third step. If the mind that has become free, and the mind that has become simple can also be empty… With the union of simplicity, freedom, and emptiness, no-mind is attained. How can the mind become empty? What is the meaning of emptiness? What is the meaning of emptiness? Emptiness means…

We are full of ourselves. We are filled with our "I" and our ego. We are obsessed with it around the clock. Search within; try it out sometimes. There is ego in the way you get up in the morning, there is ego in the way you get dressed, in the way you walk. When you build a house, it is not only for shade and shelter, in that there is also ego. You build the house so that you can make the house of your neighbor look inferior. You do not wear clothes just for the sake of covering your body. There is ego in that too; you wear them to make the clothes of others look pale in comparison. Whatever you do around the clock each day shows your ego.

There is no limit to it. Man gathers wealth to boost his ego. After all, what other interest can there be in creating wealth? Yes, money has utility, that much one can understand, but riches are gathered up to a point where they are not at all useful.

Just yesterday, I was talking about it…

A very rich man died. He was the biggest billionaire of America. He left wealth amounting to three billion dollars behind. What can be the use of three billion dollars? I mean, what can a man do with three billion dollars? Certainly, money has utility – for clothes, for food – it can be used to run your life. But what utility does three billion dollars have? You will be even more surprised; he died an unhappy man because he thought, "Only three billion?" He aimed to have ten billion.

His biographer was with him when the man was dying, and he said to him, "Sir, you must be dying a very contented man."

The rich man said, "Contented? My target was ten billion, but I was able to make only three billion. Life was over before I reached my target."

You can be sure that even if he had made ten billion, his target would have been a hundred billion – and he would have said, "Only ten?" It is just like a man who has ten rupees; he says he has only ten rupees. The man who has ten billion also says the same thing. He says, "Only ten billion?"

What utility does it have? After a certain point, the practical utility of money comes to an end, and its utility for the ego starts. Then money has no practical use, instead it is helpful to boost the ego. "The more I have, the greater a man I am." My "I" becomes that much greater, becomes that much vaster, becomes that much stronger. What else is the search for a high position other than an ego search? What else is the wish to be first in life other than an ego search? You will be surprised that the search for wealth is an ego search, and often the search for renunciation is also only an ego search. If a man who has a lot gives up everything, he talks about how much he has renounced.

Once I was visiting a monk. He would regularly say to me, "Do you know, I have renounced millions of rupees."

After he had said that three or four times, I asked him, "Can I ask you how long ago you renounced your wealth?"

He replied, "About twenty years ago."

I was a little surprised. I said, "Twenty years have gone by, and you have still not forgotten about it. It seems you did not renounce it in the right way. What is the need to remember it now? Why do you still remember that you renounced millions of rupees? Is it not that the same old ego that used to say you had millions of rupees, now says you renounced millions of rupees? Is it not that the same old arrogance, the same old ego, the same 'I' that was filled with money, is now boosted by renouncing millions of rupees? If that is so, you have wasted those twenty years. They have not been of any use to you. It appears you did not renounce it in the proper way. In your memory, you feel that you renounced millions of rupees. That money certainly has value for you even now."

What value can the money that you do not carry with you have? What utility can it have? I mean, if a man carries a million rupees with him, we can understand that it must have some use for him. A man says that he has renounced millions of rupees, and he does not carry any money with him. What is the use of remembering money that you do not carry with you at the moment? That too has a use. It has a benefit; it fulfills the ego. "Me? I renounced millions of rupees. I am greater than the people who still cling to their millions."

That is why we consider a monk greater than an ordinary man, because he renounces. If a monk also starts thinking he is greater than someone else, he has gone wrong because that is just like an ordinary man. He becomes the same old man again, because the ego has become the center of his intelligence once more.

So the question is not only about possessing wealth and position, it is also a question about renouncing wealth and position. It is not a question of what you possess, but a question of whether you are feeding your ego with it. What you have and what you do not have can both equally enhance the ego.

What you have attained and what you have renounced can both boost the ego.

Emptiness means to be empty of the ego. That is why I do not consider renouncing worldly riches real renunciation. I do not call renouncing your home renunciation. I do not call renouncing your position renunciation. That is because the very renunciation of all those things could fulfill the same purpose as the things themselves did. The only thing I call renunciation is the renunciation of the ego. I do not call giving up anything else renunciation. It is only when the ego is gone that there is renunciation.

Understand this well, because what will you do? For such a long time you have been taught that the ego is bad, the ego is sin, and the ego should be dropped. What will you do? Even if you understand that the ego is bad, what will you do? You will be caught up in trying to drop the ego, thinking that you should give up the ego. That will become a tremendous madness. Who will drop the ego? It will be the ego itself, the same old "I." Then you will be caught up in the same mistake, and it will become a case of a dog trying to catch his own tail. He jumps and the tail also jumps; then he jumps again. He is very surprised that he is not able to catch his tail – what is the matter? The more he cannot catch it, the more he starts to run around, and the harder it becomes for him. A dog cannot catch his tail, and an ego cannot destroy an ego.

Many people are eager to have the ego disappear. The more they try, the more subtle the ego becomes because of their fear; it starts moving backward. It disappears from the outside, and settles inside. An ego on the surface is far better than an ego that sits hiding inside. That is very dangerous. The one on the surface can be seen, and the one hidden inside cannot be seen. It creeps very deep inside.

An ordinary man does not have the subtlety of ego the people we call saints and holy people have. That is the reason monks all over the world cannot meet one another. There is a wall standing between them. What kind of wall? Householders have walls in their houses, one can understand that. What kinds of walls do saints, who do not even have houses, have? Householders have house walls between them. How to meet a neighbor? There is a wall in between. What kinds of walls do saints have?

Saints have more subtle walls, the walls of their egos. You can break down walls of mud and stone within half an hour, but breaking down the walls of the ego takes many lives. They take hold of you in a very subtle manner.

The ego cannot be destroyed directly. The man who gets involved in destroying the ego directly is making a mistake. The ego will become subtle, slide into the unconscious and hide inside. He will stop seeing its ways from the outside, and its roots will enter within. It will get hold of his whole soul, it will start to grip his whole soul.

Let me tell you a small story. Then you will understand what I mean by a man who is egoless. I will explain to you how egolessness can come about, and then you will understand emptiness. It happened…

A young sannyasin had been staying outside a village for some time. He was a handsome young man. A lot of people loved and respected him. He was held in high esteem and his thoughts were very influential. His visions were very revolutionary, and his life radiated great strength. One day suddenly everything changed. The same people in the village who had respected him so much set fire to his hut; the same people who had touched his feet threw stones at him, and those who had honored him started to insult him.

It happens often. Any day, the people who respect you will take revenge for it by insulting you. You should be afraid of the people who respect you because they will take revenge for it one day. Their ego has been hurt by giving you that respect. By giving you respect they have acknowledged that someone is higher than they are. That has hurt them at some deep level, and one day they will take revenge for it. Any small pretext will give them a reason to take revenge. Have great fear of the man who gives you respect because he has the potential to insult you at any moment. He can disgrace you any day. Any day he can take revenge for that respect.

Once a man came and touched my feet. I told him, "Do not touch my feet; it is dangerous."

He asked, "What is the matter?"

The danger is, he can take revenge any day. Today he touches my feet, and tomorrow, if he gets even the slightest opportunity, he will pick up a stick to break my head with.

The villagers gave the young man a lot of respect. Then one morning they all started to insult him. It happened that a girl in the village had given birth to a child, and said that the young sannyasin was the father. So naturally they started insulting him. It was absolutely natural that they would insult him. It was very natural. What was wrong in it? What the people of the village were doing was right. They took the child and brought him to the sannyasin. The young sannyasin asked, "What is the matter? What is all this?"

They said, "You ask us what the matter is? Just look at the face of this child, and then tell us what it is all about. You know very well what the matter is. If you don't know, who will know? This child is yours."

The sannyasin replied, "Is it so? Is this child mine?"

The child started to cry, and the young sannyasin began to try and soothe him and to make him stop crying. The people of the village went away after a while, and they left the child there.

It was still morning. The sannyasin took the child with him, and went to the village on his daily round of begging for food, just the way he did every day – but that day who was going to give him alms? The same people who give you millions when they respect you, will insult you by not even giving you a piece of bread. Who was going to give him bread? Wherever he went, the doors were slammed in his face. Whichever door he knocked on was slammed shut, and people told him to go away. A crowd started following him.

Perhaps no sannyasin on earth has ever gone begging for food with a child in his arms. The child kept on crying, and he went on begging. The child went on crying and the sannyasin laughed at the people who used to give him so much respect and love. Then he went to the house of the woman who had given birth to the boy. There also he called out and said, "Please do not worry about me, but at least think of this boy who is crying of hunger. Even if I am to blame for everything, this child is innocent. Why are you punishing this child for nothing? Please give him some milk."

When she saw her son in such a condition, it became very difficult for the woman to bear all this. She told her father, "Please forgive me. I told you a lie. I do not know this sannyasin at all. To save the real father from disgrace I passed the blame to this sannyasin. I thought you would only scold him a little and then come back with my child. I never imagined that things would go this far."

The members of that household became very worried about what was going on. They realized they had made a big mistake. They came running and fell at the feet of the sannyasin, and went to take the boy out of his arms.

The sannyasin asked, "What is all this? What is the matter?"

They said, "This child is not yours."

He said, "Is that so? So the boy is not mine? This morning you told me the boy was mine."

That man was egoless. The people told him, "What a madman you are! Why didn't you tell us this morning that the boy was not yours?"

He said, "What difference would it have made? The boy must be someone's; he could also have been mine" – meaning the boy must be someone's, someone has to be his father. "Now that you have already abused me, you will go and abuse someone else. What is the use? You have already burned my house, you will go and burn someone else's house too. What is the use? What difference does it make now? Everything has happened for the best. Now I know how deep your respect and love for me really is. And I know the value of anything you say. It was good that all this happened. The boy did me a great favor. Now I can see some things clearly."

They said, "You are completely mad! If you had only given us a hint that the boy was not yours, all this would not have happened."

He said, "What difference would it have made? It is only your respect for me that was torn to shreds. Am I a monk for the sake of respect? For the sake of respectability, so that I can have your respect? When I became a monk, I dropped the potential to receive honor or disgrace from you. If I had to behave in accordance with your respect and insults, what type of monk would I be?"

In reality, only a man who does not having a feeling of "I" inside is wise. The feeling of "I" does not go away directly, it goes away indirectly. How does it happen indirectly? The first part of the inner discipline to dissolve the feeling of "I" is to ask, "Who am I?" – to search for where this "I" is to be found.

Raman Maharshi has said you should ask yourself, "Who am I?" I do not tell you to ask that. I tell you to ask, "Where am I?" Search in your mind, "Where am I?" Search in your body, "Where am I?" You will not find it anywhere. If you were to sit down quietly and you searched, "Where am I?" you could keep on searching, and you would not find any point where you could say, "This is where I am." When you search inside yourself, you will not find an "I" anywhere.

There was an emperor in China called Wu. A monk named Bodhidharma went to China and when he arrived, Wu went to the border to welcome him. Wu told Bodhidharma that he had built many Buddhist temples and communes for pilgrims; had erected many Buddha statues; had given shelter to many monks and sannyasins; had opened many universities for higher learning; had given much to charity; had done so many good deeds. He asked, "What will be the fruit of all this?"

Bodhidharma said, "No reward at all; everything has been wasted. The moment you desire a reward it all goes to waste. It was neither charity nor anything else, it all became sin. Acting out of a desire for reward is sin. By asking this question, you have wasted everything. If you had remained silent, if you had neither asked anything, nor had any feeling inside to ask, there would have been great flowering."

Wu thought, "This man Bodhidharma seems to be unique. Perhaps he can do something for me." He said, "My mind is very disturbed. Can you show me a way for my mind to become peaceful?"

Bodhidharma said, "Come and see me at four in the morning, and make sure you are alone when you come. I will make everything peaceful."

On hearing this, the emperor was even more amazed. He found the monk very strange. "I have asked it of many monks and they talk a lot, but no one says he will make everything peaceful."

When he left and was going down the stairs, Bodhidharma called out to him, "Listen, make sure you bring your mind along with you. Don't leave it at home because if you come empty-handed, what will I make peaceful? Bring the mind with you and I will make it peaceful. Otherwise you can come later in the morning as usual. Some crazy people come to me and say they want to make their mind peaceful. I tell them they can come, and they come empty-handed. They don't bring the mind with them. So you had better bring your mind with you."

Wu was even more surprised. He thought, "When I come back, naturally my mind will come with me. Why does he mean by saying that?"

In the early morning, he kept thinking about it on the way there. The moment he arrived, Bodhidharma asked him, "Did you bring it? Did you bring your mind?"

Wu asked, "What are you talking about? My mind is part of me."

Bodhidharma said, "Then close your eyes and search for it. Where is it? If you can find where the mind is, I will make it peaceful. If you cannot find the mind, what can I do?"

The emperor searched a great deal. As he closed his eyes and searched, he noticed he could not find any mind anywhere. He searched and searched, but there was no mind, there was only total silence. He opened his eyes and said, "I am in great difficulty. There is absolutely nothing to be found."

Bodhidharma said, "It has become peaceful. How can that which cannot even be found be disturbed?"

In fact, you have never gone inside and looked. Your being outside yourself is the origin of your mind. If you go inside and search, there is no mind. Your being outside yourself is the origin of your "I." If you go inside and search, there is no "I," there is no "me"; it is the shadow of your being outside. Since you are constantly moving outside yourself twenty-four hours a day, a shadow is born, and that gives you the impression of an "I."

You must have noticed that when you walk on the road, a shadow follows you. Do you think that the same shadow that starts following you the moment you take the first step on the road is still behind you after an hour?

It is not the same shadow following you. The shadow goes on changing every moment. How can the same shadow follow you? New rays keep falling on you from moment to moment, and a new shadow keeps forming every moment. You move an inch, and a new shadow forms. It is not the same shadow you saw in the beginning. If you walk for an hour, a new shadow forms every second. After an hour, you say your shadow has been following you. That statement is totally false. It is not the same shadow. The shadow keeps renewing itself every moment. No shadow is following you. When you stand in the sun, a shadow is formed every moment. If you walk ahead, a new shadow will be formed; if you move further ahead, another shadow will be formed; if you move still further, a third shadow will be formed. If you keep moving further, shadows will keep on forming. There is no shadow following you.

In the same way, in the outside world we are constantly active in the activities of daily life. In that activity, a shadow is formed that constantly changes. We cannot see its constant change, and an illusion is born that it is "I." The illusion of "I am," the feeling of "I am," is the shadow that is born from our interaction with the outside world. We start clinging to the "I."

Search inside, and you will not find any "I" there. No matter how much you search, you cannot find any "I" there. There is no shadow. There is no activity. There is no relationship with anyone. There is no sun through which a shadow can be formed. You come out of the house and a shadow is formed. You go into the house and the shadow disappears.

A man roams around outside for an hour. If he then goes inside the house and says, "A shadow is still following me," and asks me to tell him where it is, I will tell him there is no shadow inside the house. The shadow is only outside the house.

The very feeling of "I" or "me" is a shadow born through the relationship with others. Only when I see you, do I feel you are there. When I see you, I feel you are there. When I see the whole world, I see that all the people are there and because of them, I am also there. The shadow feeling of the "I" is born because of the "you." Where there is a "you," there is an "I," but if I go inside myself, there is no "you." When there is no "you," how can there be an "I"?

Do you understand what I am saying? When the "I" is in front of a "you," because of the "you," the feeling of "I" is born. If I go inside, there is no "you." When there is no "you," how can an "I" be born? In the absence of a "you," the "I" is not born.

There is no "I." We spend our whole lives outside ourselves, so we feel there is an "I." We start to grow a shadow, an "I" that is completely imaginary, an "I" that was born due to "you," born out of reacting to "you," a shadow that was born from relationships on the outside. It should have a high position, it should have a lot of wealth, it should have a big house, it should have this, and it should have that. We spend our whole life maintaining an "I" that is completely imaginary and false, that is only an echo of the "you."

We are bound to fail. If a man puts clothes on his shadow, if a man builds a house for his shadow, if a man collects wealth for his shadow, he will find in the end that there is no shadow, and everything has been left behind. Then the sorrow and anguish that take hold of his mind, that is the suffering, his discontentment; that is the failure and frustration.

What I am saying is, go inside the shadow "I" that was born from the "you," and take a look. Do not ask, "Who am I?" Ask, "Where am I?" You will search and find out that "I" am nowhere. If "I" am nowhere, a transformation will take place in your life; all the ways to fulfill that "I" will appear to be futile. Earning a position for the "I," collecting wealth for the "I," and even the act of renouncing for the "I" will be meaningless. It is futile to do anything for something which does not exist.

There is nothing more untrue, there is nothing more illusory, and there is nothing more false than the "I." There is nothing more illusory than the "I." The "I" is the only illusion there is.

If the "I" disappears, if you cannot find it, what happens? What you then perceive is the truth, is the soul, is godliness. When the shadow, the "I" disappears, what you perceive is the truth. It is your self-nature, it is your authentic being, your ultimate being, your soul.

To erase the "I," there is no need for you to change your clothes, to renounce wealth. Rather, what is needed is to search whether the "I" is there or not. If the "I" that you are going to drop is not there at all, dropping it is madness. You only have to know if the "I" is there or not there. If there is no "I," there is no question of dropping it.

That is why I say there is no question of dropping the ego. The one who drops it will be filled with a more solid ego. He is fighting with a shadow, isn't he? He is fighting with something that is not there. What is not there cannot be defeated by fighting it. He will be defeated by what is not there.

Please try to understand what I am saying. If you fight with what is not there, you are bound to be defeated because what is not there cannot be defeated. In the end, you will find that you have lost. It is futile to fight with something that does not exist. What is really needed is to know whether the "I" is there or not. Before you start thinking you can be egoless, you should know where the ego is. Is it anywhere?

Those who search peacefully inside find there is nothing inside. In meditation, in peacefulness, in simplicity of mind, the ego cannot be found. When nothing can be found, a transformation takes place in life. The same daily behavior that was based upon the ego becomes based upon the ultimate reality. All doing was centered around the ego. When that center dissolves, the world changes. People become different. Another person is born, and his daily activity starts to go toward the ultimate reality. Then the ego is not the center, then the ultimate reality, the soul, existence, is the center. Then what he does is not for the fulfillment of the ego; it is only a gift of the soul, it is only a sharing of the being, it is only a dispersal, a diffusion.

Ego collects, non-ego shares. I call charitable all those actions that come from egolessness. No charity can be in actions that are filled with the ego. They are all demands; someone demands something. Someone with an ego demands something, and someone with no ego shares. That is why as long as you have a sense of ego, you cannot be charitable. Your charity will only be a demand. If you build a temple, you will think that you will be rewarded in heaven for that action. If you feed a monk, or give alms to a monk, in your mind you will feel you should be rewarded in your next birth for the virtue of that action. Whatever you do, if you renounce something, in your mind you will feel you should achieve liberation. As long as you have any residue of the ego in you, no matter what you do, there will always be a demand behind it. Behind it you will always be motivated by profit, behind it there will always be a motive to gain something.

Until the ego ends, there is no charity. Only when there is no ego can you do charitable deeds. Then whatever you do will be a charitable deed, because the very thing that demands is no longer present. There is only letting go and sharing. That is what I call the feeling of being empty. The feeling of emptiness is sannyas. The emptiness of the "I" is the third step. When you search for the "I," you will find that the "I" is not there; the "I" is empty.

This is how I have talked to you about the three steps: freedom of consciousness, simplicity of mind and emptiness of mind. If all those three jewels can find a place in your life, something will be born out of their combination, and that is called enlightenment. Enlightenment is the door to truth. Enlightenment is the door to the self. Enlightenment is the door to supreme life. Only through enlightenment will you come face-to-face with ecstasy, with light, and with bliss.

It is only after attaining enlightenment that someone becomes grateful and blessed. Someone who has not attained it can be presumed to be dead; someone who has not attained it can be considered to be in the grave. A person who has not attained it should understand that he is already in the grave. His life is worthless. His life is completely meaningless. It has no meaning. It is of no worth; there is no gratitude in it.

What I call religion is the way to bring your life toward meaningfulness and gratitude. Religiousness means to attain enlightenment. Religiousness and enlightenment are the same thing. Religiousness is the very self-nature itself, and through enlightenment the perception, the encounter, and the experience of it takes place.

Blessed are those few people who attain enlightenment. Only they are alive, the rest of the people do not exist. They are only shadows. Those who believe in shadows are only shadows. The one who believes in reaction, in arrogance, and in ego is only a shadow. Don't believe in shadows. Don't cling to shadows.

There are two ways of clinging to the shadow. Someone who indulges in sensual pleasures looks for pleasures for the shadow. And the ascetic who makes arrangements for renunciation is in reaction to the indulgence of sensual pleasures. Both are mad. If something is only a shadow, neither indulgence of it is meaningful, nor is renunciation of it meaningful.

By knowing the shadow, the shadow disappears. There is neither indulgence nor renunciation, neither clinging nor dropping. It is the state that has been called beyond both indulgence and renunciation. Where there is attraction, there is belief in the shadow; where there is renunciation, there is also belief in the shadow. The man who collects wealth believes in wealth; the man who renounces wealth also believes in wealth. The man who runs after women believes in women, and the man who runs away from women also believes in women. Both are believers. One is inclined toward attraction, and the other is averse to attraction. One runs after the shadow and the other runs away from the shadow, but both believe in the shadow. They believe in the "I" that is not there. Both are wrong. Only the man who is beyond all attractions and aversions is right.

That means that when there are no attractions and no aversions, the shadow has been scattered. Neither do you have to follow someone, nor do you have to escape from anything. There is no one to run after, nor anyone to run away from. The man who runs after something is running away from himself; the man who runs away from someone is also running away from something in himself. The man who neither runs after something, nor runs away from something, is rooted in his self. To be rooted in oneself is truth; to be in oneself is religiousness; to be in oneself is to be in the soul; to be in oneself is to attain godliness.

These are the few things I have talked about in the last three days. Maybe some of the words I have spoken will turn into seeds in you. It is possible that some words may sprout inside you. Something may become a vision for you; I pray to existence that it will become a vision for you.

I am very thankful to all of you for listening to my talks with such love and such peace. Finally, I bow down to the buddha within you. Please accept my greetings.

About Osho

Osho's unique contribution to the understanding of who we are defies categorization. Mystic and scientist, a rebellious spirit whose sole interest is to alert humanity to the urgent need to discover a new way of living. To continue as before is to invite threats to our very survival on this unique and beautiful planet.

His essential point is that only by changing ourselves, one individual at a time, can the outcome of all our "selves" – our societies, our cultures, our beliefs, our world – also change. The doorway to that change is meditation.

Osho the scientist has experimented and scrutinized all the approaches of the past and examined their effects on the modern human being and responded to their shortcomings by creating a new starting point for the hyperactive 21st Century mind: OSHO Active Meditations.

Once the agitation of a modern lifetime has started to settle, "activity" can melt into "passivity," a key starting point of real meditation. To support this next step, Osho has transformed the ancient "art of listening" into a subtle contemporary methodology: the OSHO Talks. Here words become music, the listener discovers who is listening, and the awareness moves from what is being heard to the individual doing the listening. Magically, as silence arises, what needs to be heard is understood directly, free from the distraction of a mind that can only interrupt and interfere with this delicate process.

These thousands of talks cover everything from the individual quest for meaning to the most urgent social and political issues facing society today. Osho's books are not written but are transcribed from audio and video recordings of these extemporaneous talks to international audiences. As he puts it, "So remember: whatever I am saying is not just for you...I am talking also for the future generations."

Osho has been described by *The Sunday Times* in London as one of the "1000 Makers of the 20th Century" and by American author Tom Robbins as "the most dangerous man since Jesus Christ." *Sunday Mid-Day* (India) has selected Osho as one of ten people – along with Gandhi, Nehru and Buddha – who have changed the destiny of India.

About his own work Osho has said that he is helping to create the conditions for the birth of a new kind of human being. He often characterizes this new human being as "Zorba the Buddha" – capable both of enjoying the earthy pleasures of a Zorba the Greek and the silent serenity of a Gautama the Buddha.

Running like a thread through all aspects of Osho's talks and meditations is a vision that encompasses both the timeless wisdom of all ages past and the highest potential of today's (and tomorrow's) science and technology.

Osho is known for his revolutionary contribution to the science of inner transformation, with an approach to meditation that acknowledges the accelerated pace of contemporary life. His unique OSHO Active Meditations™ are designed to first release the accumulated stresses of body and mind, so that it is then easier to take an experience of stillness and thought-free relaxation into daily life.

Two autobiographical works by the author are available:

Autobiography of a Spiritually Incorrect Mystic, St Martins Press, New York (book and eBook)

Glimpses of a Golden Childhood, OSHO Media International, Pune, India (book and eBook)

Osho International Meditation Resort

Each year the Meditation Resort welcomes thousands of people from more than 100 countries. The unique campus provides an opportunity for a direct personal experience of a new way of living – with more awareness, relaxation, celebration and creativity. A great variety of around-the-clock and around-the-year program options are available. Doing nothing and just relaxing is one of them!

All of the programs are based on Osho's vision of "Zorba the Buddha" – a qualitatively new kind of human being who is able *both* to participate creatively in everyday life *and* to relax into silence and meditation.

Location
Located 100 miles southeast of Mumbai in the thriving modern city of Pune, India, the OSHO International Meditation Resort is a holiday destination with a difference. The Meditation Resort is spread over 28 acres of spectacular gardens in a beautiful tree-lined residential area.

OSHO Meditations
A full daily schedule of meditations for every type of person includes both traditional and revolutionary methods, and particularly the OSHO Active Meditations™. The daily meditation program takes place in what must be the world's largest meditation hall, the OSHO Auditorium.

OSHO Multiversity

Individual sessions, courses and workshops cover everything from creative arts to holistic health, personal transformation, relationship and life transition, transforming meditation into a lifestyle for life and work, esoteric sciences, and the "Zen" approach to sports and recreation. The secret of the OSHO Multiversity's success lies in the fact that all its programs are combined with meditation, supporting the understanding that as human beings we are far more than the sum of our parts.

OSHO Basho Spa

The luxurious Basho Spa provides for leisurely open-air swimming surrounded by trees and tropical green. The uniquely styled, spacious Jacuzzi, the saunas, gym, tennis courts…all these are enhanced by their stunningly beautiful setting.

Cuisine

A variety of different eating areas serve delicious Western, Asian and Indian vegetarian food – most of it organically grown especially for the Meditation Resort. Breads and cakes are baked in the resort's own bakery.

Night life

There are many evening events to choose from – dancing being at the top of the list! Other activities include full-moon meditations beneath the stars, variety shows, music performances and meditations for daily life.

Facilities

You can buy all of your basic necessities and toiletries in the Galleria. The Multimedia Gallery sells a large range of OSHO media products. There is also a bank, a travel agency and a Cyber Café on-campus. For those who enjoy shopping, Pune provides all the options, ranging from traditional and ethnic Indian products to all of the global brand-name stores.

Accommodation

You can choose to stay in the elegant rooms of the OSHO Guesthouse, or for longer stays on campus you can select one of the OSHO Living-In programs. Additionally there is a plentiful variety of nearby hotels and serviced apartments.

www.osho.com/meditationresort
www.osho.com/guesthouse
www.osho.com/livingin

Books by Osho in English

Early Discourses and Writings
The Art of Living
Astrology
Breaking All Boundaries
Compassion and Revolution
A Cup of Tea
Dimensions beyond the Known
Earthen Lamps
The Eternal Quest
Flowers of Love
From Sex to Superconsciousness
The Great Challenge
Hidden Mysteries
I Am the Gate
The Independent Mind
Into the Void
Keys to a New Life
Life Is a Soap Bubble
Love Letters to Life
New Dimensions of Yoga
The Path of Meditation
The Psychology of the Esoteric
Religion's Expiration Date
The Search for Peace
Seeds of Wisdom
Silence: The Message of Your Being
Work Is Love Made Visible
Three Steps to Awakening
Into the Void

Meditation
And Now and Here
In Search of the Miraculous
Meditation: The Art of Ecstasy
Meditation: The First and Last Freedom
The Inner Journey
The Perfect Way

Buddha and Buddhist Masters
The Book of Wisdom
The Dhammapada: The Way of the Buddha(Vols 1-12)
The Diamond Sutra
The Discipline of Transcendence (Vols 1-4)
The Heart Sutra

Indian Mystics
Bliss:Living beyond Happiness and Misery (Shiv Sutras)
Die O Yogi Die (Gorakh)
Enlightenment: The Only Revolution (Ashtavakra)
Krishna: The Man and His Philosophy
Showering without Clouds (Sahajo)
The True Name (Vols 1&2) (Nanak)
The Last Morning Star (Daya)
The Song of Ecstasy (Adi Shankara)

Baul Mystics
The Beloved (Vols 1 & 2)

Kabir
The Divine Melody
Ecstasy: The Forgotten Language
The Fabric of Life
The Fish in the Sea Is Not Thirsty
The Great Secret
The Guest
The Path of Love
The Revolution

Jesus and Christian Mystics
Come Follow to You (Vols 1-4)
I Say Unto You (Vols 1 & 2)
The Mustard Seed
Theologia Mystica

Jewish Mystics
The Art of Dying
The True Sage

Western Mystics
Guida Spirituale (*Desiderata*)
The Great Challenge (Treatise of St. Dionysius)
The Hidden Harmony (Heraclitus)
The New Alchemy: To Turn You On (Mabel Collins' *Light on the Path*)
Philosophia Perennis (Vols 1 & 2) (*The Golden Verses of Pythagoras*)
Reflections on Kahlil Gibran's *The Prophet*
Theologica Mystica
Zarathustra: A God That Can Dance (Nietzsche's *Thus Spake Zarathustra*)
Zarathustra: The Laughing Prophet (Nietzsche's *Thus Spake Zarathustra*)
The Voice of Silence (Mabel Collins' *Light on the Path*)

Sufism
Just Like That
The Perfect Master (Vols 1 & 2)
The Secret
Sufis: The People of the Path (Vols 1 & 2)
Unio Mystica (Vols 1 & 2)
Until You Die
The Wisdom of the Sands (Vols 1 & 2)

Tantra
Tantra: The Supreme Understanding
The Tantra Experience: The Royal Song of Saraha (same as Tantra Vision, Vol. 1)
Tantric Transformation: The Royal Song of Saraha (same as Tantra Vision, Vol. 2)
The Book of Secrets: Vigyan Bhairav Tantra

The Upanishads
Behind a Thousand Names (Nirvana Upanishad)
Finger Pointing to the Moon (Adhyatma Upanishad)
Flight of the Alone to the Alone (Kaivalya Upanishad)
The Heartbeat of the Absolute (Ishavasya Upanishad)
I Am That (Isa Upanishad)
The Message beyond Words (Kathopanishad)
Philosophia Ultima (Mandukya Upanishad)
The Supreme Doctrine (Kenopanishad)
That Art Thou (Sarvasar Upanishad, Kaivalya Upanishad, Adhyatma Upanishad)
The Ultimate Alchemy (Vols 1 & 2) (Atma Pooja Upanishad)
Vedanta: Seven Steps to Samadhi (Akshaya Upanishad)
The Way beyond Any Way (Sarvasar Upanishad)

Tao
The Empty Boat

The Secret of Secrets
Tao: The Golden Gate (Vols 1 & 2)
Tao: The Pathless Path (Vols 1 & 2)
Tao: The Three Treasures (Vols 1-4)
When the Shoe Fits

Yoga

Yoga: The Science of the Soul (Vols 1-10)
-The Path of Yoga (Vol.1)
-The Heart of Yoga (Vol.2)
-Yoga: The Mystery beyond Mind (Vol.3)
-The Alchemy of Yoga (Vol.4)
-Yoga: A New Direction (Vol.5)
-Essence of Yoga (Vol.6)
-Yoga: The Science of Living (Vol.7)
-Secrets of Yoga (Vol.8)
-Yoga: The Path to Liberation (Vol.9)
-Yoga: The Supreme Science (Vol.10)

Zen and Zen Masters

Ah, This!
Ancient Music in the Pines
And the Flowers Showered…
And the Grass Grows By Itself…
A Bird on the Wing
Bodhidharma: The Greatest Zen Master
The Buddha: The Emptiness of the Heart
Christianity, the Deadliest Poison and Zen, the Antidote to All Poisons
Communism and Zen Fire, Zen Wind
Dang Dang Doko Dang
The First Principle
God Is Dead: Now Zen Is the Only Living Truth
The Great Zen Master Ta Hui
Hsin Hsin Ming: The Book of Nothing
I Celebrate Myself: God Is No Where, Life Is Now Here
Kyozan: A True Man of Zen
The Language of Existence
Live Zen
The Miracle
Nirvana: The Last Nightmare
No Mind: The Flowers of Eternity
No Water, No Moon
One Seed Makes the Whole Earth Green
The Original Man
Returning to the Source
The Search: Talks on the 10 Bulls of Zen
A Sudden Clash of Thunder
The Sun Rises in the Evening
Take it Easy
This. This. A Thousand Times This
This Very Body the Buddha
Turning In
Walking in Zen, Sitting in Zen
The White Lotus
Yakusan: Straight to the Point of Enlightenment
The Zen Manifesto: Freedom from Oneself
Zen: The Diamond Thunderbolt
Zen: The Mystery and the Poetry of the Beyond
Zen: The Path of Paradox (Vols 1-3)
Zen: The Quantum Leap from Mind to No-Mind
Zen: The Solitary Bird, Cuckoo of the Forest
Zen: The Special Transmission

Osho: On the Ancient Masters of Zen

Dogen: The Zen Master
Hyakujo: The Everest of Zen – With Basho's haikus
Isan: No Footprints in the Blue Sky
Joshu: The Lion's Roar

Ma Tzu: The Empty Mirror
Nansen: The Point of Departure
Rinzai: Master of the Irrational

Responses to Questions
Be Still and Know
Beyond Enlightenment (Talks in Bombay)
Beyond Psychology (Talks in Uruguay)
Come, Come, Yet Again Come
From Bondage to Freedom
From Darkness to Light
From Death to Deathlessness
From Ignorance to Innocence
From Misery to Enlightenment
From Personality to Individuality
From the False to the Truth
From Unconsciousness to Consciousness
The Goose Is Out
The Great Pilgrimage: From Here to Here
The Invitation
Light on the Path (Talks in the Himalayas)
My Way: The Way of the White Clouds
Nowhere to Go but In
The Osho Upanishad (Talks in Bombay)
The Path of the Mystic (Talks in Uruguay)
The Razor's Edge
Sermons in Stones (Talks in Bombay)
Socrates Poisoned Again After 25 Centuries (Talks in Greece)
The Sword and the Lotus (Talks in the Himalayas)
Transmission of the Lamp (Talks in Uruguay)
Walk without Feet, Fly without Wings and Think without Mind
The Wild Geese and the Water
Yaa-Hoo! The Mystic Rose
Zen: Zest, Zip, Zap and Zing

Osho's Vision for the World
The Golden Future
The Hidden Splendor
The New Dawn
The Rebel
The Rebellious Spirit

The Mantra Series
Hari Om Tat Sat
Om Mani Padme Hum
Om Shantih Shantih Shantih
Sat Chit Anand
Satyam Shivam Sundaram

Personal Glimpses
Books I Have Loved
Glimpses of a Golden Childhood
Notes of a Madman

Interviews with the World Press
The Man of Truth: A Majority of One

For any information about OSHO Books, please contact:

OSHO Media International
17 Koregaon Park, Pune – 411001, MS, India
Phone: +91-20-66019999 Fax: +91-20-66019990
E-mail: distribution@osho.net
Website: http://www.osho.com

For More Information

For a full selection of OSHO multilingual online destinations, see osho.com/allaboutosho

The official and comprehensive website of OSHO International is osho.com

For more OSHO unique content and formats see:

- OSHO Active Meditations: osho.com/meditate
- iOsho, a bouquet of digital OSHO experiences featuring OSHO Zen Tarot, TV, Library, Horoscope, eGreetings and Radio. Please take a moment to do a one time registration which will allow you a universal login. Registration is free and open to anyone with a valid email address: osho.com/iosho
- The OSHO online shop: osho.com/shop
- Visit the OSHO International Meditation Resort: osho.com/visit
- Contribute in the OSHO Translation Project:oshotalks.com
- Read the OSHO Newsletters: osho.com/NewsLetters
- Watch OSHO on YouTube: youtube.com/user/OSHOInternational
- Follow OSHO on Facebook: facebook.com/osho.international.meditation.resort
- and Twitter: twitter.com/OSHO

Thank you for buying this OSHO book.